A Feast of Scotland

A Feast of Scotland

Janet Warren

LOMOND BOOKS

The author and publishers wish to acknowledge the generous help of The Drambuie Liqueur Company in the publication of this book.

First published in Great Britain in 1979 by
Hodder and Stoughton Ltd

This edition published in 1990 by
Treasure Press for Lomond Books
Michelin House
81 Fulham Road
London SW3 6RB

Reprinted 1992, 1993

ISBN 1 85051 112 8

Printed in Hong Kong

Contents

The Meal of Ceremony 81

Food for Kings 107

Now Let the Cheering Cup Be Poured 153

Note to American readers

In the recipes, measures are given in British imperial units (e.g. pints) followed by their American equivalents in brackets. Below is a list of British ingredients and cooking terms and their American counterparts.

Anchovy essence	Use anchovy paste
Ashet	Meat dish
Bacon rashers	Bacon slices
Bannock	Flat, round cakes
Baking tray	Cookie sheet
Beetroot	Beets
Belly of pork	Pork arm steak
Bicarbonate of soda	Baking soda
Biscuits	Crackers/cookies
Blaeberries	Bilberries (raspberries or blueberries can also be used)
Blind pie case	Empty pie shell (line shell with foil and dried beans – which can be used again – and bake for specified time)
Blood heat	Lukewarm (98.6°F)
Boiling fowl	Stewing fowl
Broad beans	Use fava, lima or java
Cake mixture	Cake batter
Case	Pie shell
Caster sugar	Use granulated sugar
Cheddar, Scottish	Cheddar, American
Chilli	Chili pepper
Chipolata sausages	Cocktail sausages
Cornflour	Cornstarch
Creamed (potatoes)	Mashed
Crisps	Potato chips
Demerara sugar	Light brown sugar
Digestive biscuits	Graham crackers
Double cream	Whipping cream
Dripping	Meat drippings
Essence	Extract
Farls	Quarters
Farola	Use milled wheat or semolina
Fats	Shortening
Frying pan	Skillet
Gelatine	Gelatin
Girdle	Griddle
Girnel	Canister or meal chest
Glacé angelica	Candied angelica
Glacé cherries	Candied cherries
Goblet (of liquidizer)	Bowl or container (of blender)

Golden syrup	Substitute light corn syrup
Greaseproof paper	Vegetable parchment
Green cured bacon	Unsmoked bacon
Grill, a	Broiler
Grill pan	Broiling pan
Grill, to	Broil
Gut (fish)	Clean
Haricot beans	Navy or white beans
Hodgils	Oatmeal dumplings
Icing	Frosting
Icing sugar	Confectioners' sugar
Jam	Preserves
Jelly bag	Use several layers of cheesecloth
Joint (of meat)	Roast of meat
Kail	Kale
Kippers	Kippered herrings
Kitchen paper	Paper towels
Knead/knock back (dough)	Punch down
Knuckle of veal	Veal shanks
Lettuce, a	Head of lettuce
Liquidizer/Mixer	Blender/Mixer
Middle neck of lamb	Neck of lamb
Minced beef (mince)	Ground beef
Mince, to	Grind
Mixed spice	Allspice
Mushroom ketchup	Use marinated mushrooms with added walnuts
Nut (of butter)	Pat
Packet puff pastry	Prepared puff pastry
Pickled pork	Cured pork
Pigeon	Squab
Pinhead oatmeal	Irish oatmeal
Plain flour	All-purpose flour
Pluck	Substitute a selection of organ meats
Polythene	Plastic wrap
Preserve	Preserves
Preserving sugar	Substitute granulated sugar
Prove	Rise
Pudding	A steamed, baked or boiled dish, most often sweet but also meat- or vegetable-based
Pudding basin	Pudding mold or ovenproof bowl
Pudding cloth	Cheesecloth
Rasher of bacon	Slice of bacon
Ratafia biscuits	Substitute almond flavoured cookies or dried macaroons

Salt beef	Corned beef brisket
Scrag end neck of lamb	Neck of lamb
Self-raising flour	All-purpose flour sifted with baking powder
Seville oranges	To each quart of sliced naval/Florida oranges add one lemon sliced thin
Shredded suet	Chopped beef suet
Sieve, to	Sift
Single cream	Light cream
Soft brown sugar	Use light brown sugar
Spring onion	Scallion/green onion
Spurtle	Wooden spoon or spatula
Stalk	Remove stalks
Stewing steak	Braising beef
Stick celery	Celery stalk
Stoned raisins	Seedless raisins
Streaky bacon	Use regular bacon
Strong plain flour	Unbleached white flour
Sultanas	Seedless white raisins
Tartlet tin	Muffin pan
Top and tail (gooseberries)	Clean
Treacle	Molasses
Vegetable mill	Food mill
Whisk	Beat/whip
Wholemeal	Wholewheat

METRIC CONVERSION TABLE

All recipes are given in imperial measures, with American equivalents in brackets.

The following tables give approximate conversions from imperial to metric measures, rounded up or down.

Weights		Measurements	
$\frac{1}{2}$ oz	10 g (grams)	$\frac{1}{8}$ in	3 mm (millimetre)
1	25	$\frac{1}{4}$ in	$\frac{1}{2}$ cm (centimetre)
$1\frac{1}{2}$	40	$\frac{1}{2}$	1
2	50	$\frac{3}{4}$	2
$2\frac{1}{2}$	60	1	2.5
3	75	$1\frac{1}{4}$	3
4	110	$1\frac{1}{2}$	4
$4\frac{1}{2}$	125	$1\frac{3}{4}$	4.5
5	150	2	5
6	175	3	7.5
7	200	4	10
8	225	5	13
9	250	6	15
10	275	7	18
12	350	8	20
1 lb	450	9	23
$1\frac{1}{2}$	700	10	25.5
2	900	11	28
3	1 kg 350 g	12	30

Volume

2 fl oz	55 ml
3 fl oz	75
5 fl oz ($\frac{1}{4}$ pint)	150
$\frac{1}{2}$ pint	275
$\frac{3}{4}$ pint	425
1 pint	570
$1\frac{3}{4}$ pints	1 litre
(2 pint basin = 1 litre)	

Introduction

Scotland is remarkable for the wide variety of good
produce that can be gleaned from the land and its
surrounding waters, despite the fact that barely a
quarter of Scottish soil is under cultivation. The deep
seas offer an almost endless choice of fish, from the
smallest sprat to the splendid turbot, and the craggy
coastline with its many estuaries and deep inlets yields a
wealth of delicate shellfish. The beautiful rolling
moorlands are the home of feathered game, while up in
the mountains red deer run wild, feasting on moss and
lichen. The higher you climb in search of them, the
sweeter will be the venison. Here, too, is the home of
the mountain hare, and bees colonize the heather to
provide delicious heather honey. Plump trout and other
river fish inhabit the fathomless lochs and unpolluted
burns, while salmon leap their way majestically up river
to their traditional spawning grounds. Sheep and prime
beef cattle graze on the aromatic herbs of the uplands,
and the lowlands offer rich pastureland to Scotland's
famous dairy herds. The climate is not always a kindly
one, but the soil yields copious crops of oats and barley,
cereals which provide a healthy basis to the Scottish
diet.

With such native riches no elaborate treatment is
required to make the most mouthwatering of meals.
From the humblest of origins the art of Scottish cookery
has developed over the centuries to achieve international
renown. Foreign influence has played a large and
beneficial part in the development of the Scottish
culinary repertoire, but it has never been able to destroy
its essential nature.

In Celtic times the sea was understandably held in
religious awe. The eating of fish was forbidden, as they
were held to be sacred to the pagan goddess Venus, and
this must have made the diet far more frugal than
necessary. But by the eleventh century Catholicism had
taken a universal hold, and the vast fishing grounds of
coasts, rivers and lochs began to be exploited. Fresh
water fish included carp, tench, and of course the king
and queen of river fish, salmon and trout. So plentiful
were they that as early as the thirteenth century Scottish
salmon was pickled and exported to London, where it
was considered to be a food for the poor! The sea was

rich in herring and mackerel, whiting, haddock, cod, turbot, and the smaller sprats and smelts, to mention only some. Shellfish were plentiful, particularly cockles, mussels and enormous oysters. Only a century ago the glorious oyster beds in the Firth of Forth made Edinburgh the city of oysters, but sadly here and elsewhere the beds have been destroyed by pollution and overfishing. Lobsters and scallops were abundant in the Orkneys, and in time these were exported to Germany. So important did the harvesting of the sea become that coastal towns sprang up and thrived or fell with the fluctuation of fish stocks. Scots fishermen found they had to contend with the Dutch, who were only too efficient at reaping their waters, and this led to blows in the fifteenth and seventeenth centuries. Nowadays through diplomatic channels we are fighting to preserve fishing limits around our Scottish coasts, because overfishing by Icelandic, Scandinavian and other North European countries has caused a dangerous depletion in fish stocks.

Fish supplies are seasonal, and methods had to be found of preserving such a valuable commodity. Kippering is done mostly on the west coast, where the

The Cock of the Wood. An early engraving of the native grouse.

best herring are to be found, but a lot of the smoking industry is centred around Aberdeen on the east coast. The famous Findon haddock are cured in the village of that name to the south of Aberdeen, and to the north whitings are dried in the wind and moistened with sea-water during the curing process to produce speldings. The famous Arbroath Smokie was also developed in this area, although it started life in nearby Auchmithie. Smoke pits were dug out of the ground and the haddock were tied in pairs and hung for smoking over halved whisky barrels. There are two types of smoking: hot smoking actually cooks fish such as smokies and buckling, so they are ready for the table when they leave the smoking kiln; while fish that are cold smoked, like finnans and kippers, need to be cooked before eating. The stronger the cure, the longer the fish will keep. The basic cures have not changed since fisherwomen in coastal villages cured and smoked the fish themselves over peat and seaweed fires, but home curing became illegal in the nineteenth century, and much of the industry moved to new factories in Aberdeen itself, contributing greatly to the prosperity of that town.

The practice of salting and curing fish and meat was probably introduced to Scotland from Scandinavia by the Viking raiders and so, it is thought, were the splendid Aberdeen Angus cattle, source of much of the succulent Scotch beef. In general, however, the Scots were not great meat eaters in the past, and livestock was kept mostly for wool, milk and eggs, not finding its way to the stockpot until it was old and rather tough, when long, slow cooking methods were necessary. The autumn was the time for the killing and salting of meat for the winter, and the delicious mutton hams are a speciality shared by Scotland and Scandinavia. Beef and venison were cured in the same way, and smoked Solan goose was a delicacy of the breakfast table. Pigs were kept for food only in the border areas, where recipes for pickling pork survive. Nowadays, however, Ayrshire bacon enjoys a deservedly high reputation. The plentiful game birds of the moors and mountains were often spurned by country folk in the poorest of homes, who seemed happy to exist on a mainly vegetarian diet.

Facing page: A miniature version of the copper still traditionally used in the making of Drambuie and a selection of some of the principal ingredients: various herbs and a blend of the finest mature whiskies

Pigeons were a useful source of meat in towns, and every burgh had its own rabbit warren.

The staple food of the Scottish table was grain, chiefly oats and barley, augmented by kail and by the wild vegetables, fruits and herbs which could be reaped from fields and hedgerows. Raspberries, strawberries and gooseberries are all native to Scotland, as is the blaeberry and the Christmas cranberry. Vegetables might include wild spinach, carrots and nettles. Oats are a nourishing food, and the physical and mental energy of the Scot have frequently been attributed to the large amount of oatmeal he consumes. Only now are we once again beginning to realise the value of unrefined foodstuffs.

Early cooking methods were simple. The fuel for the fire was usually peat, and over this would be hung the bakestone, which was superseded by the grid-iron, and the kail-pot. The former, which is still very much part of the Scottish kitchen, is a round, flat, cast-iron plate with a hooped handle. It took the place of the oven, and on this was baked the daily bread, which of course was unleavened. The term 'breed' covered bannocks, scones and oatcakes. The flour was coarse, and corn was ground in a hand-mill called a quern. This method was used well into the last century in some of the islands. The kail-pot was also made of iron, and was a large round saucepan with a lid and three legs. It stood over the fire and simmered the broses and broths which formed the daily menu. Sometimes it was buried in smouldering peat and used as an oven. Such long, slow cooking produces the most flavoursome dishes.

Hardly anyone possessed a built-in oven, and it was the abbeys and monasteries which were among the first to do so. During the eighteenth century the kitchen range became a widespread acquisition, but before this it was the custom to take the day's baking to the public bakehouses in these religious establishments, which were such a focal point in community life. The abbey gardens were the first to introduce cultivated fruit trees to Scotland, and some of the best varieties of apple and pear trees were said to have been imported from France in this way.

Scotland has long had a special relationship with

Left: Haggis

An eighteenth-century painting by David Allan showing couples dancing the highland fling to the accompaniment of bagpipes

France, and has often turned to her for support in skirmishes with England. Although strong links go back to the twelfth century, it was during the sixteenth century that the 'Auld Alliance' between the two countries really brought about a change in culinary fashions. James V of Scotland married a French noblewoman, Mary of Guise-Lorraine, and she brought with her to the court at Holyrood in Edinburgh a large retinue of her own servants and courtiers. Entertaining in the French manner became all the rage, and fashionable people vied with one another to follow her lead and set the most lavish table. The fashions set by Mary of Guise-Lorraine were strengthened by her daughter Mary, the beloved Queen of the Scots, who had been brought up at the French court. Everybody connected with court circles now wanted a French chef, and their tables overflowed with a wasteful abundance of rich food. These extravagances led to a real food shortage, and in 1581 a law had to be passed to prevent 'superfluous banquetting'. Dishes were allotted according to one's station in life, and fines were imposed if these regulations were contravened. During

A domestic scene near Moffat, 1795. Painting by David Allan

this century the practice of eating dessert was introduced from France. Before this sweet and savoury dishes had been served side by side. Now the guests would remove to a separate room for this new course. Imported French wines were drunk with the meal, and it was followed by French brandy.

These culinary fashions were at first confined to Edinburgh and its environs, and it was not until the eighteenth century that elaborate cooking became the vogue in wealthier houses throughout Scotland, not always to the liking of some of the more conventional lairds! Although the direct association with France came to an end with the unification of the English and Scottish parliaments in 1707, French influence is still apparent in many areas of Scottish life today – in the laws and the language as well as in the kitchen. Many words associated with food and its preparation have their counterpart in French rather than English, words like gigot or jiggot, from *gigot*, a leg of mutton; ashet from *assiette*, a meat dish; grosert, the gooseberry, from *groseille*. The Scot will say of a tasteless dish 'it hae no gout' (pronounced goo), which derives from

Grouse shooting

the French *goût*, meaning taste.

It was during the seventeenth century that Scotland's most famous product was properly developed. I refer, of course, to whisky. *Aqua vitae* was in fact distilled in religious establishments as early as 1494, but it was not until much later that the practice became widespread in the Highlands. Before this the Highlander drank either the fresh burn water, or milk and its by-products, such as buttermilk and whey. Ale was drunk in the lowlands and wine was brewed from the native fruits and plants. French wines were of course drunk at table where they could be afforded, but heavy duties were in time imposed on these and their consumption was necessarily limited. To compensate for this a clause in the law allowed families to distil sufficient whisky in their own homes for the needs of the household, a woolly sort of regulation that invited abuse. The surplus barley would be malted and turned into *uisge-beatha* (the Gaelic for 'water of life') in a pot-still over a peat fire. Clansmen would carry scallop shells with them to use as tumblers for their whisky, and drank it copiously. So rapidly did home distilling spread throughout Scotland that whisky

assumed a great importance in the Scottish economy
and was used as barter for rent, servants' wages and
general purchases. After the Union with England in
1707 the English parliament imposed excise duty on it,
but this led to an even greater increase in illicit distilling
and consumption. The illegal product had to be quickly
disposed of, and the obvious solution was to drink the
surplus. By the eighteenth century it was established as
the standard drink for morning, noon and night, and
was used on every possible occasion, for purposes
ranging from the medicinal to the ceremonial. It is
probably just as well that tea was introduced to
Scotland at that time, and by the end of that century
had replaced whisky at least as a breakfast and
afternoon beverage!

Scotland's Drambuie liqueur is based on whisky and
has an intriguing history dating from this period. In
1746 *Bliadhna Theàrlaich* or Charlie's Year, as the
Highlanders called it), the Young Pretender to the
English throne, Bonnie Prince Charlie, was forced to flee
to the Western Islands after the defeat of his army at
Culloden. On Skye he was given shelter and hospitality
by the Mackinnons of Strathaird, and having no other
gift with which to thank the family for harbouring him
at risk to themselves, the Prince gave them the recipe
for his personal liqueur. The family treasured the secret
formula for 150 years, making up small quantities of the
delicious drink for their own pleasure and the annual
gathering of the clan. Early this century the young
Malcolm Mackinnon, an astute businessman with his
own whisky company, persuaded his kinsmen to hand
over the recipe for the secret essence. In an Edinburgh
cellar he experimented with jelly bags and copper pans
to get the liqueur exactly right. It was then a formidable
task to get his new drink tried and accepted by
conservative wine merchants, and ironically it was the
First World War which brought success to the company.
Homesick Scotsmen began to order this native drink for
their regimental messes, and by the end of the war
production had become a major enterprise. The recipe
has remained a closely guarded secret within the
Mackinnon family, and today the essence is prepared by
Mrs Norman Mackinnon in her own home outside

A view of Edinburgh today showing Princes Street, the National Gallery and, on the far left, Edinburgh Castle

Edinburgh, from where it is taken to the modern blending laboratory to be blended with the finest malt whiskies. Its name is taken from the Gaelic *an dram buidbeach*, the drink that satisfies.

Drambuie has achieved international renown as one of the most successful liqueurs, and it is a tribute to the quality of this and so many of its fellow Scottish drinks and foodstuffs that they will be found on the shelves of every good grocer and wine merchant in the British Isles. On the sophisticated delicatessen counter, alongside the best of continental groceries, you will find butter rich shortbread and the humble oatcake, almond-strewn Dundee cake, Keiller marmalades, Scottish jellies and jams and melting heather honey, huge sides of smoked salmon and a selection of Scottish cheeses. The butcher's counter will yield choice cuts of prime Scotch beef, small plump grouse, colourful braces of pheasant and haunches of venison in season; and the New Year will see the first of the tender mountain lamb. A tempting array indeed of the feast of Scotland.

A Furthy Meal

Breakfast is a splendid affair in Scotland, the meal in which traditional recipes and local produce really come into their own. It reached its peak as a meal of some grandeur in the late eighteenth century, when it was customary wherever it could be afforded to find the table laden not only with the famous fresh and cured fish, but also with a selection of cold and smoked meats – venison, beef and the delicious mutton hams which are a speciality; with cheeses and eggs; with bannocks, oatcakes, heather honey, currant jellies and marmalades; and of course a dish of porridge. Up until then the meal would have been accompanied by whisky or other spirits, but at about this time tea came into favour as a breakfast drink. Breakfast was often preceded by a stomachic of Highland bitters – whisky infused with spices and bitter herbs.

Nowadays when one thinks of a Scottish breakfast porridge and kippers come to mind, and indeed porridge or brose has been a staple dish for rich and poor alike since time immemorial. There is a fine difference between porridge and brose. The latter is made by pouring hot water onto oatmeal, and even today some shepherds carry a small bag of meal and mix themselves a bowl of brose with fresh burn water. Porridge, on the other hand, is traditionally made by sprinkling the meal onto boiling water, a handful at a time, and stirring with a spurtle, a special wooden porridge stick. Many legends surround this national dish, and such was the importance of grain in the Scottish diet that students were granted a half-term holiday to enable them to go home and refill their sack of meal. This holiday was known as Mealy Monday and is still celebrated annually in Scottish universities. Tradition has it that porridge was always eaten standing up, so that the clansmen were ready when called to arms by their chief.

The popular kipper is only one of many deliciously cured fish for which Scotland is renowned. A little about the history of curing will be found in the Introduction, and the various treatments of the common herring are a tribute to the resourcefulness of the Scot, each region having developed its own speciality. At the present time there is a herring shortage, and this once

The kitchen of the Georgian House, 7 Charlotte Square, Edinburgh

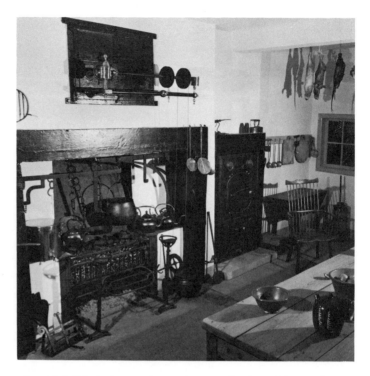

plentiful fish is becoming a luxury for breakfast. The most sought after are from Loch Fyne, and 'wastlin' herrin'', or west coast herrings, were and still are much appreciated in other parts of Scotland and the British Isles. Loch Fyne herrings were known as Glasgow Magistrates or Baillies because of the plumpness of their bellies. So important is the herring to the Scottish diet that rivalry between Dutch and Scottish fishing fleets has more than once led to blows, and in 1650 Cromwell introduced a law decreeing that only herring carried in British ships could be handled in our ports. Towns have prospered and declined due to the fluctuation of fish stocks, and in AD 64 the Bishop of East Anglia built a church dedicated to the herring so that men could pray for the success and health of the herring fishermen. The kipper is the most famous form of smoked herring but red herring are also cured whole in two different processes: as bloaters, which are dry salted and cold smoked; and as buckling, which are hot smoked and therefore ready to eat. The strong salty flavour of these fish has made them a popular export to the Mediterranean; in Britain a milder cure is preferred, and

*The harbour of Gourdon,
Kincardine*

these have been developed now that we have other
methods of preserving the fish. The other smoked fish
greatly favoured at the breakfast table is the haddock,
which is transformed by curing into the delicate Finnan
Haddie and the less well-known Arbroath Smokie.

Just as the shepherd would make his bicker of brose,
so the soldier would carry a bag of oatmeal and a metal
bakestone behind his saddle and make his own oatcakes
over the camp fire. The simple bakestone was replaced
at home by the girdle, or grid-iron, and over this were
baked the first unleavened bannocks and scones, made
with a coarse, hand-ground flour. As ovens were
acquired and refined flour became available the Scottish
housewife developed her baking talents for the tea and
breakfast table, but the modest Scottish oatcake remains
an unsurpassable delight. Local heather honey is always
found on the breakfast table, and jams and jellies,
together with the marmalades which originated in
Scotland, complete the repast, of which Dr Johnson
justifiably commented: 'If an epicure could remove by a
wish in quest of sensual gratification, wherever he had
supped, he would breakfast in Scotland.'

*Facing page: Fraserburgh
fishermen bringing in the catch*

Porridge

'The halesome parritch chief o' Scotia's food', as Robbie Burns described porridge, is traditionally referred to in the plural. They are served with cream, milk or buttermilk. The porridge should be served in a bowl made of hard wood and eaten with a horn spoon which does not conduct the heat. Each person takes a spoonful of porridge from the communal bowl and dips it into his own dish of milk. Nowadays, however, the accompaniments are more often than not poured over the porridge.

Serves 4

2 pints cold water (5 cups)

4 oz medium oatmeal ($\frac{2}{3}$ cup)

Bring the water to a rapid boil then slowly sprinkle over the oatmeal, stirring it with the spurtle constantly. If the oatmeal is added too quickly it will form lumps (knots) and make the porridge unpleasant to eat. Stir the porridge until it returns to the boil then cover the pan and simmer it slowly for about 30 minutes, stirring frequently, or until it is of a thick pourable consistency. Salt, about $\frac{1}{2}$ teaspoon, is always added to porridge but not until at least 10 minutes after it has been simmering or it could tend to harden the meal.

Grilled Herrings

allow 1 herring per person, preferably with soft roe

2–3 oz melted butter (4–6 tablespoons)

salt and pepper

Remove the heads and gut the fish, reserving the roes (the fishmonger will do this for you if liked). Wash the fish well then sprinkle the inside with seasoning, brush with melted butter and replace the roes. Slash the fish two or three times at intervals of about 1 inch on each side, then brush the skin with butter.

Place the fish on a greased grill pan and cook slowly for about 20 minutes, basting frequently and turning at least once during the cooking time.

Serve the cooked herrings with toast.

Herrings in Oatmeal

Serves 4

4 herrings, cleaned

4 oz medium oatmeal ($\frac{2}{3}$ cup)

2 level teaspoons salt

a good pinch of pepper

a little fat for frying

Although I have suggested serving this dish at breakfast, which is the custom in Scotland, herring cooked in this way are also delicious for lunch accompanied by a mustard sauce (see page 58).

Using a sharp knife continue the cut on the underside of the fish along to the tail. Lay the herring cut side on the table and bang it across the backbone in three places using either the side of your hand or a rolling pin. Turn the fish over and ease out the bone, removing as many of the smaller bones as possible at the same time.

Mix the salt and pepper with the oatmeal, put it onto a plate and coat each herring on both sides, pressing the seasoned oatmeal firmly into the fish.

Heat a little fat in the frying pan and put in the fish two at a time skin side upwards, so that they need only be turned once. Fry over a brisk heat until lightly brown on one side, then turn them over and cook the other side (they will take 5–7 minutes in all).

Drain the fish on kitchen paper and serve with lemon and parsley sprigs.

The smokie industry in Arbroath. The haddock are cured hanging in pairs by the tail

Kippers

Kippers are fresh herrings split and cleaned and immersed in vats of salt for a few minutes. The fish are then smoked over smouldering oak chippings for about eight hours. The result is a delicately flavoured, thick and fleshy fish suitable for breakfast, lunch or supper.

There are several ways of cooking kippers. Personally I prefer them grilled.

To grill

Wipe the fish and remove the head and fins. Brush with a little melted butter on both sides and also brush the rack of the grill. Cook the fish under a pre-heated grill for about 3 minutes on each side. Brush the fish with more butter as it cooks. It will be ready when the backbone starts to come away from the flesh.

Serve the fish with a pat of butter and freshly made brown toast.

To fry

Melt about 1 oz (2 tablespoons) butter in a pan, prepare the kippers as for grilling, then fry them for about 3 minutes on each side or until crisp and cooked. It is best to cook the fish with the skin side upwards first so that it only needs to be turned once. When the kipper is ready serve it on a warm plate with the remaining butter in the pan poured down the centre.

Jug method

The advantages of this method of cooking kippers are that it does not require constant attention and that it lessens the lingering smell kippers sometimes leave after cooking.

Prepare the kipper as for grilling, push a skewer through the tail and suspend the fish in a deep jug. Fill the jug with boiling water and leave it for 5 minutes, by which time the fish should be cooked. Drain and serve with a pat of butter in the centre.

Finnan Haddock

Finnan or Findon Haddock are named after the hamlet of Findon near Aberdeen where this particular way of curing haddock was first practised. The heads are removed and the haddocks cleaned and split open, then sprinkled with salt and left for a couple of hours or more. The fish are then hung to dry in the open for about three hours before being smoked over peat or hardwood sawdust until they are a rich, golden colour, which takes up to twelve hours.

Finnan Haddock are best eaten within a day of curing. They are cooked and served in many ways and make either a marvellous breakfast dish or a tasty meal for lunch or supper.

To grill

Brush the fish on both sides with melted butter, butter the rack of the grill also, then place the fish skin side upwards on the grill pan. Cook the fish for about 5 minutes then turn it over, brush with more butter and grill the other side. Serve with 2 lightly poached eggs. Sufficient for 2 people.

To bake

Wash the fish and place it in a roasting tin. Cover with water and lay 3 or 4 onion rings on top. Bake at Gas 4/350°F/180°C for 20–30 minutes. While the fish is cooking, scramble 2 eggs. Serve them with the drained fish and complete the meal with sippets of toast.

To poach

Trim the haddock and place it in a shallow pan. Cover with water, add a bayleaf and some peppercorns, and slowly bring the liquid to the boil. Reduce the heat, cover the pan and simmer the fish for 3 minutes or until tender. Drain and serve with a knob of butter in the centre.

Kedgeree

Serves 4–6
6 tablespoons long grain rice
2 Finnan haddock
2 oz butter ($\frac{1}{4}$ cup)
squeeze of lemon juice
pinch of grated nutmeg
pinch of cayenne pepper
pinch of salt
5 hard boiled eggs

This recipe comes from Overscaig, on Loch Shin in Sutherland. Overscaig was originally a coaching inn with a horse change station for coaches. It was also a drover's halt when sheep were driven from the crofts in the North West to the Lairg market, and wool was taken by road and loch to the railhead. Since the nineteenth century Overscaig has been renowned as a fishing centre for the great lochs of the glens running from Laxford to Bonar-Bridge. The cooking is done by Sheila Hamilton-Hesse, who runs the hotel with her husband Jimmy. Most of the produce is local, with the emphasis on seafood. Here is her recipe for kedgeree.

Boil the rice in plenty of salted water until cooked. Poach the haddock, skin and bone it and flake it roughly. Melt the butter in a large saucepan and add the fish, rice, lemon juice and seasoning. Heat gently, stirring lightly. Chop three of the hard boiled eggs and mix in at the last minute, before piling onto a hot dish and garnishing with the two remaining eggs, also chopped.

Arbroath Smokies

This succulent way of curing a haddock originated from a fishing village near Arbroath named Auchmithie. In the early nineteenth century the inhabitants moved to Arbroath, taking their skills with them, and by the beginning of this century the Smokie industry had vastly developed. Unlike Finnan Haddock Smokies are cured closed, tied in pairs by the tail.

To prepare the fish for serving

Heat the smokies on both sides under a grill or in a moderate oven. Open them up carefully and remove the backbone. Spread lavishly with butter and freshly milled black pepper then close up and heat for a few minutes more.

Served piping hot, they make an extremely welcome breakfast dish accompanied by toast and butter.

Facing page: Drambuie Marmalade

Cured Meats

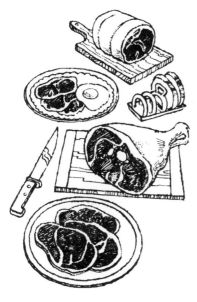

Pork was never a popular meat in Scotland, particularly in the Highlands, as the pig was regarded as a dirty animal. However, the famous Ayrshire bacon cannot be bettered. The cure is a rather succulent and sweet one that is still used in many hamlets around the country, although Ayrshire bacon is now readily available at butchers and grocers. Serve the bacon boiled as a joint and sliced when cold, or slice it while it is raw and grill the rashers until golden.

The other and more unusual cured meat is Mutton Ham. As the name suggests it is mutton cured and smoked in a method rather similar to that used for pork. In the Highlands the ham is served cold for breakfast although it is also served hot as a luncheon or supper dish with caper sauce (see Boiled Mutton on page 62).

The cure involves steeping a large leg of mutton in a mixture of saltpetre, cooking salt, brown sugar, allspice, black pepper and coriander seeds for about a fortnight, turning the meat daily. It is then smoked over peat or a hard wood fire for ten to fourteen days, and finally soaked for two hours before boiling. This cure can also be used for goose or beef.

Left: Breakfast sideboard laid with Baps, Aberdeen Butteries, Porridge, Kippers and Ayrshire Bacon

Girdle Scones

Makes 8

8 oz plain flour (2 cups)

a pinch of salt

2 level teaspoons cream of tartar

1 level teaspoon bicarbonate of soda

2 oz margarine ($\frac{1}{4}$ cup)

1 standard egg (size 3)

about 5 tablespoons milk

Sift the flour, salt, cream of tartar and bicarbonate of soda into a bowl, rub in the margarine, and when it is evenly distributed bind the mixture together with the egg and enough milk to make a soft but not sticky dough.

Turn the dough onto a lightly floured surface and roll it into a 9-inch circle. Cut it into eight pieces.

Heat a girdle evenly then grease it lightly with a little lard. Place the scones on it and cook them for about 15 minutes in all, turning them halfway through the cooking time.

Serve girdle scones warm for breakfast.

Oatcakes

The art of making good oatcakes is to work quickly. Although the ingredients seem very simple the mixture can be difficult to handle as it is slightly wet. Always make sure the surface and your hands are well covered with meal whenever you work the dough.

This recipe makes two bannocks each of 8 inches in diameter or eight farls, which are bannocks cut into quarters.

Serve oatcakes with butter, honey and marmalade for breakfast or as an accompaniment to broth or cheese for lunch. They are also delicious served with herrings for high tea or supper.

8 oz medium oatmeal (1⅓ cups)
a good pinch of salt
1 tablespoon dripping or lard
¼ teaspoon bicarbonate of soda
about 3 fl oz hot water
(6 tablespoons)

Mix the oatmeal, salt and bicarbonate of soda together. Melt the dripping and pour it into the centre, then stir in enough hot water to make a stiff dough (use the spurtle or porridge stick for this task).

Turn the dough onto a well mealed surface and knead it thoroughly. Divide the dough into two. Press each half out with well mealed hands and roll it into 8-inch circles. Trim the edges using a plate as a guide. The finished dough should be about a quarter of an inch in thickness. Sprinkle the surface with meal and cut into farls if desired. Cook the oatcakes on a girdle set over a medium heat or in a heavy-based frying pan. They should take about 3 minutes and are ready when the edges start to curl. Rub the surfaces with a little more oatmeal then place under the grill to crisp and slightly brown.

Alternatively the oatcakes can be baked in an oven at Gas 3/325°F/160°C for about 30 minutes.

Traditionally oatcakes are stored buried in oatmeal in a girnel or meal chest: however they do keep very well in an airtight tin. Reheat them in a moderate oven for a few minutes before serving.

Quick Rolls

Makes 8

8 oz plain flour (2 cups)

a pinch of salt

½ level teaspoon bicarbonate of soda

1 level teaspoon cream of tartar

½ oz margarine (1 tablespoon)

¼ pint milk (⅔ cup)

a little beaten egg for glaze

Sift the flour, salt, bicarbonate of soda and cream of tartar into a bowl. Add the fat and rub it in. Bind the ingredients together with the milk to make a soft dough. Turn it onto a floured surface and knead it until smooth. Divide the dough into eight and roll each piece into a ball.

Place the rolls on a greased baking tray, brush them with egg glaze, then bake at Gas 5/375°F/190°C for 15 minutes or until golden brown.

Baps

Makes 8

1 lb strong plain white flour (3½–4 cups)

a pinch of salt

1 oz fresh yeast (1 cake compressed yeast)

1 level teaspoon caster sugar

½ pint milk and water mixed (1¼ cups)

2 oz lard (¼ cup)

a little extra flour

Baps are the traditional morning roll in Scotland. They seem to appear only on the breakfast table and are best eaten warm from the oven.

Sift the flour and salt into a bowl. Warm the milk and water then stir in the yeast and sugar so they dissolve.

Rub the lard into the flour, then make a well in the centre, pour in the yeast liquid and mix the ingredients together to form a dough. Turn the dough onto a lightly floured surface and knead it for about 5 minutes until smooth.

Put the dough into a lightly oiled bowl, cover it with oiled polythene and leave the dough in a warm place to prove. It should have doubled in bulk in 30 minutes. Turn the dough onto a lightly floured surface and knead it back to its original size, then cut it into eight and knead each piece into a round. Flatten the rounds with a rolling pin and place them on floured baking trays. Leave the trays in a warm place to prove for about 15 minutes.

Brush the surface of each with water and dust with flour, then bake the baps at Gas 7/425°F/220°C for 15–20 minutes or until golden brown. Cool on a wire tray.

Aberdeen Butteries

Also called Buttery Rowies, these rolls are said to originate from the French croissant, but although they are very similar in taste the shape is completely different. They are associated with Aberdeen where the fishing fleets used to take them out; the high fat content kept the fishermen warm as they worked in rough seas.

Makes 18

1 lb strong plain flour (3½–4 cups)

½ oz fresh yeast (½ cake compressed yeast)

1 teaspoon caster sugar

8 oz butter (1 cup)

4 oz lard (½ cup)

½ pint tepid water (1¼ cups)

Sift the flour into a bowl. Dissolve the sugar in the water then crumble in the yeast and mix it until smooth. Stir the liquid into the flour to form a dough, then turn it onto a floured surface and knead the dough until smooth. Place it in a clean bowl, cover the surface with a sheet of greased polythene then leave the dough in a warm place to prove for about 45 minutes or until doubled in bulk.

Knock the dough back. Beat the two fats together and divide them into three portions. Roll the dough out into an oblong and dot the top two thirds with one portion of the fat. Fold the bottom third up over the middle third and the top third down over the other two thirds and seal the edges. Leave to rest in a cool place for 30 minutes then repeat the process twice more, giving the dough a quarter turn each time and leaving it to rest after each rolling.

Divide the dough into 18 ovals and place them on greased baking trays, spacing them a little apart as they will rise. Prove them in a warm place for 30 minutes, then bake them at Gas 6/400°F/200°C for 20–25 minutes or until well risen and golden brown.

Brown Breads

Here are two recipes for wholewheat loaves. The first is the traditional recipe using yeast, but the second is a useful and less time-consuming method of making a delicious loaf for breakfast.

Wholewheat Bread

Makes 1 large and 2 small loaves

2 oz fresh yeast (2 cakes compressed yeast)

2 level tablespoons brown sugar

1½ pints warm water (3¾ cups)

1 level dessertspoon salt (2 teaspoons)

3 lb wholewheat plain flour (10½–12 cups)

1 oz butter (2 tablespoons)

a little beaten egg for glaze

Crumble the yeast into ½ pint (1¼ cups) of warm water and stir it together with 1 teaspoon of sugar until all is dissolved.

Rub the butter into the flour, mix in the salt, then pour in the remaining warm water with the yeast liquid and mix the ingredients together to form a soft dough.

Turn the dough onto a floured surface and knead it for about 5 minutes or until the surface is smooth. Put the dough into a large greased bowl, cover it with polythene and leave the bowl in a warm place for the dough to prove. It should take about 45 minutes to double in bulk. Then turn the dough out onto the working surface and knock it back gently until it becomes its original size.

To shape the loaves divide the dough in half. Divide one half in half again. Taking one piece of dough at a time, roll or punch it into a rectangle that measures the length of the tin and three times the width, then fold the dough into three. Turn the loaf over so that the join is underneath, then drop it into the well greased tin, turning the ends slightly under to give the loaf a rounded top.

Beat a little salt into the egg glaze and brush some over the surface of the loaf. Prove it again, this time for about 20 minutes or until it stands just above the rim of the tin. Bake the loaves at Gas 8/450°F/230°C for 20 minutes, then reduce the heat to Gas 6/400°F/200°C. The small loaf will take a further 15 minutes and the large loaf 25 minutes. The loaves will be cooked when they are well risen and golden brown and sound hollow when tapped on the base.

Cool slightly before serving.

Speedy Wholemeal Loaf

Makes 1 large loaf

1 level dessertspoon golden syrup (2 teaspoons)

1 teaspoon lemon juice

7½ fl oz warm water (1 cup)

8 oz wholemeal plain flour (2 cups)

8 oz white plain flour (2 cups)

a good pinch of salt

1 level teaspoon bicarbonate of soda

1 level teaspoon cream of tartar

¼ pint milk (⅔ cup)

a 2-lb loaf tin, greased

Dissolve the golden syrup in the water, add the lemon juice and leave to cool.

Sieve the plain white flour into a bowl with the salt, bicarbonate of soda and cream of tartar. Mix in the wholemeal flour. When the liquid is cool stir it into the dry ingredients with the milk, to make a fairly wet consistency. Turn the dough into the tin and spread it to the sides, hollow out the centre slightly, then bake the loaf at Gas 6/400°F/200°C for 15 minutes. Reduce the heat to Gas 4/350°C/180°C for a further 20–30 minutes or until the bread is golden brown and well risen.

Cool on a wire tray then keep for a day before cutting.

Marmalades

Two legends testify to the Scottish origins of marmalade. It was apparently created by Janet Keiller in the early eighteenth century after her husband bought a vast quantity of cheap Seville oranges from a Spanish ship which took refuge from a storm in Dundee harbour. They were of course too bitter to eat, and Mrs Keiller thriftily made them into the orange jam which was to become a world famous conserve and an essential part of every British breakfast table. A more romantic tale has the beloved Queen of the Scots, Mary, on the point of death from a chill caught while riding through a wet night to meet her lover Bothwell. Her French chef created a sweet concoction of quinces or oranges to tempt her appetite. She liked it so much that a dish was kept always at her bedside, and thus took the name 'Marie malade'.

Orange Jelly Marmalade

Makes about 6 lb

3 lemons

Seville oranges to make a total weight of fruit of 4 lb

5 pints water (12½ cups)

about 4 lb sugar

½ oz butter (1 tablespoon)

Wipe and stalk the fruit. Chop or coarsely mince the oranges and lemons then put them into a pan with the pips, add the water and bring it to the boil. Cover the pan then simmer the fruit for about 1–1½ hours or until it is soft. Pour the marmalade into a scalded jelly bag and leave the juice to drip through overnight.

Next day measure the juice and allow 1 lb sugar to each pint (2 cups per 2½ cups liquid) (at this stage do not be tempted to squeeze the jelly bag to get out the last few drips as it will cause the jelly to go cloudy).

Put the juice and sugar into a preserving pan. Dissolve the sugar over a low heat, then bring the jelly to the boil and boil it rapidly for about 15–20 minutes or until setting point is reached (see Thick Cut Marmalade). Stir in the butter. Pour the jelly into clean warm jars, cover, label and store.

Drambuie Marmalade

Makes 7 lb

2 large sweet oranges

1 lemon

1 grapefruit

4½ pints water (11¼ cups)

5 lb preserving sugar (10¼ cups)

2 tablespoons Drambuie

Remove the rind only from the fruits and chop it coarsely or finely as liked. Cut the fruits in half, remove the pips and as much of the pith as possible, then chop the fruit roughly and put it into a bowl with the rind, water and a muslin bag containing the pips and pith. Cover the marmalade and leave overnight to soak.

Next day turn the ingredients including the bag of pips into a large pan, bring to the boil, cover and simmer for about 1½ hours or until the rind is very soft. Remove the bag of pips and squeeze out as much liquid as possible back into the marmalade.

Stir in the sugar and when every grain has dissolved boil the preserve to setting point (see Thick Cut Marmalade). Add the Drambuie, then leave the marmalade to cool for 10 minutes before pouring it into clean, warm jars. Cover, label and store until required.

Thick Cut Marmalade

Makes 11–12 lb

3 lb Seville oranges

2 medium sweet oranges

8¼ pints water (21 cups)

about 7 lb preserving sugar
(15¾ cups)

a little butter

Wipe all the oranges and put them into a large pan with 8 pints (20 cups) water. Bring to the boil, cover the pan and simmer the fruit for 1½–2 hours or until really soft.

Drain the oranges, keeping the liquid, then cut each fruit into four and scrape out the flesh. Put the pips and excess pith from the skins into a separate bowl. Shred the skins and add with the flesh to the liquid in which the fruit was cooked. Put the pips and pith into a small pan with the remaining ½ pint water and simmer for 15 minutes, then strain this liquid into the marmalade.

Rub the inside of a preserving pan with butter. Measure the marmalade into the preserving pan and add 1 lb sugar for every 1 pint of marmalade (2 cups per 2½ cups liquid), then dissolve the sugar over a low heat. When every grain has melted bring the marmalade to the boil and boil it rapidly for about 30 minutes or until setting point. To test for set, place a little marmalade onto a plate. When it is cold, run your finger through the surface and see if it wrinkles. If it does not, boil the marmalade for a little longer. Leave to stand for 15 minutes after it is ready then pour into clean, warm jars, cover, label and store until required.

Hamely Fare

Any traveller visiting a Scottish household will be overwhelmed by the warmth of his welcome and the abundance of good food set before him because the Scots, above all, are a hospitable people, and offer the very best of their resources to their guests. Yet the family table at midday might in contrast be quite frugal. Clan warfare, together with the loss of plots of land and grazing rights because of the practice of enclosing the estates, has in the past led to considerable poverty. And so with typical resourcefulness the Scottish housewife has turned her hand to concocting wholesome and flavoursome dishes out of the most meagre of provisions. Nowadays in a time of greater prosperity she has never quite lost this sense of thrift, tending for example to use cheaper cuts of meat than her English counterpart, and many of Scotland's splendid national dishes, created out of necessity, have survived on their own merit.

Until the eighteenth century few vegetables were grown, although time has proved the suitability of Scotland's soil to a wide variety of produce. Up until that time each household possessed its kail-yard, and little else was grown, apart from cabbage and perhaps a few leeks. Gooseberries grew in abundance, and if one was prepared to search for wild fruits strawberries, raspberries and cranberries could be found, and a large crop of bilberries, together with wild spinach, roots and delicious herbs such as thyme and garlic. The Highlanders liked to gather nettles for their soups and in coastal areas certain types of seaweed were used in soups and sauces. This in fact has medicinal properties and is now dried and sold in health food shops. The potato was introduced from Ireland in the eighteenth century and the turnip from Holland, giving rise to the Tatties-an'-Neeps which are the customary accompaniment to Haggis. The wealthier households now began to develop their own kitchen gardens, and by the nineteenth century this had become a fashionable practice and a splendid variety of produce was grown. The humbler folk, however, preferred to confine themselves to their unimaginative kail-yards. The delicious vegetable concoctions described in this chapter will show the ingenuity with which the modest kail,

Queen Victoria and Prince Albert picnicking at Carn Lochan in 1861

cabbage and potato were treated.

Most main dishes were prepared in the kail-pot, and long slow cooking over the open peat fire produced some delicious and nourishing main meal broths, similar in nature to the French *pots au feu*. This was the best way of tenderising meat, too, because sheep, cattle and poultry were kept primarily for their wool, milk and eggs, so they were a little old by the time they reached the cooking pot! When the broth was ready the meat would be removed and served separately with a sauce while the stock and vegetables made a sustaining first course or a separate meal. Recipes vary not only from region to region but from family to family, each housewife having her own versions of the favourites which would be handed down from mother to daughter. In the coastal areas substantial soups would be made in the same way with fish.

Fish have been an important part of the Scottish diet since the eleventh century, and an important export, too. Shellfish used to be abundant, particularly cockles, mussels and oysters. The latter were so plentiful in the

A country blacksmith offers simple hospitality to his elegantly dressed visitors

past that they were used to flavour meat dishes, but sadly the famous oyster beds have long been fished dry and the rivers polluted. And when land was short for the grazing of cattle and sheep, the delicious game birds, hares and rabbits were there for the taking by country folk, and many a humble table was graced with what have now become luxury foods.

The Scottish family puddings have evolved from the sweet-savoury boiled puddings of the eighteenth century, in which dried fruits were added to the meat to give a more piquant flavour. Cloutie puddings were boiled in a cloth and were served on special occasions only, or in wealthy establishments where the expensive dried fruits and spices could be afforded. With the discovery of proper raising agents these were no longer necessary to lighten the puddings, and they can now be made from more modest ingredients.

Facing page: A crofter's living room, reconstructed in the Highland Folk Museum, Kingussie

Brose

This very traditional porridge soup dates back to early days when the shepherd or labourer would carry a wooden or leather hoggin filled with dry ground oats. Some time during the day he would fill the hoggin with water from a brook, sling it again on his back and continue with his work. The warmth and movement of his body plus, no doubt, the bacteria in the hoggin, would set up a fermentation which would result, some hours later, in a thick and slightly aerated liquid. Nowadays the brose is made much more quickly.

Allow a handful of oatmeal per person. Put it into a bowl with a knob of butter, add a little salt and pour over enough boiling water to cover. Stir it well and leave for a few minutes to allow the oatmeal to swell, although it should still be raw in the centre. Serve with cream or sweet milk.

The word brose is nowadays associated with a number of different broths, such as Kail Brose which follows, or Mussel Brose, both of which are thickened with oatmeal.

Kail Brose

Almost every region of Scotland has its own version of this national dish. It is important to have a really flavoursome stock for this recipe.

Serves 6
3 pints good stock (7½ cups)
2 oz oatmeal (¼ cup)
salt and pepper
1 lb curley kail

Bring the stock to the boil, add the oatmeal and leave it to simmer while you prepare the kail.

Remove all the coarse stems. Shred the leaves finely and wash them thoroughly. Drain the kail and add it to the pan, then simmer the brose for about half an hour or until the kail is tender. Leave the pan uncovered so as to retain the colour of the vegetable.

Serve piping hot.

Cullen Skink

A traditional recipe from the shores of the Moray Firth. The word 'skink' comes from the Gaelic, and means 'essence'.

Serves 4–6

1 Finnan haddock ($\frac{1}{2}$–$\frac{3}{4}$ lb)

1 large onion, sliced

1 pint milk (2$\frac{1}{2}$ cups)

about 1 lb potatoes, cooked and mashed

salt and pepper

$\frac{1}{2}$ oz butter (1 tablespoon)

1 level dessertspoon chopped parsley (2 teaspoons)

Put the haddock into a shallow pan and add just enough cold water to cover. Bring it to the boil, add the onion and simmer for about 5 minutes until cooked. Lift the fish from the pan. Remove all the skin and bones, put them back into the stock and cook the stock for an hour.

Meanwhile break the fish into flakes. When the stock is ready strain it, add the milk and bring to the boil, then stir in the fish and simmer for 5 minutes. Finally stir in enough potato to make a creamy soup, check for seasoning and add the butter in small pieces. Just before serving scatter the chopped parsley over the soup.

Mussel Broth

This soup is based on a recipe that is often served for lunch with bread or toast.

Serves 4

1 quart fresh mussels (3 cups)

$\frac{1}{4}$ pint dry cider ($\frac{2}{3}$ cup)

6 peppercorns

bouquet garni (a sprig of parsley and thyme plus a bay leaf tied together with string)

1$\frac{1}{2}$ oz butter (3 tablespoons)

1 large onion, finely chopped

1 garlic clove, crushed

1 oz plain flour ($\frac{1}{4}$ cup)

1$\frac{1}{2}$ pints fish stock (3$\frac{3}{4}$ cups)

1 tablespoon freshly chopped parsley

Wash the mussels well and scrub them, removing all the weed and discarding any cracked shells or ones that stay open when tapped. Using a small knife scrape off the dark 'beard' from each, then put the mussels into a pan and add the peppercorns, bouquet garni, and cider. Cover the pan and over a high heat, shaking the pan occasionally, cook the mussels for 5 to 7 minutes or until they have opened. Any that remain closed, discard.

Remove the mussels from their shells, then keep them covered in a bowl and strain the liquid into another bowl, leaving to settle. Melt the butter in a pan, add the onion and garlic and sauté the ingredients until they are soft but not coloured. Stir in the flour then carefully blend in the fish stock. Add the mussel stock also, being very careful not to disturb the dregs just in case they are gritty. Stir the soup until it boils, then add the mussels and adjust the seasoning.

Stir in the parsley before the soup is to be served.

Red Pottage

Serves 4–6
4 oz haricot beans (⅔ cup)
2 sticks celery, chopped
1 cooked beetroot, peeled and chopped
1 onion, peeled and chopped
3 tomatoes, chopped
2 pints stock (5 cups)
1 oz butter (2 tablespoons)
chopped mint

Cover the beans with cold water and leave to soak overnight.

Next day drain the beans, melt the butter in a large pan and add the beans and all the vegetables. Fry the ingredients for 5 minutes, stirring occasionally, then pour in the stock and add seasoning to taste. Bring to the boil and simmer covered for 3 hours or until the beans are very soft.

Remove the beetroot then rub the pottage through a sieve, reheat, check the seasoning and serve garnished with chopped mint.

Scottish Cheddar Cheese Soup

Serves 6
2 onions, thinly sliced
2 oz butter (¼ cup)
2 oz flour (½ cup)
1 pint white stock or water (2½ cups
pinch of pepper
6 oz Scottish Cheddar cheese, grated (1½ cups)

This is a recipe from Toravaig House Hotel, a small family hotel at Knock Bay in the south or garden of Skye, five miles south of Armadale. In 1773 Dr Johnson and Mr Boswell stayed on Skye with the Mackinnons (the family to whom Bonnie Prince Charlie gave the recipe for Drambuie). Their visit could be regarded as the beginning of the tourist trade on which the island is now so dependent for its livelihood. The cuisine of Toravaig House Hotel is run by the son of the owners, Mr and Mrs Grant Abernethy. Another delicious recipe from Toravaig is Cabbie Claw on page 59.

Melt the butter in a saucepan and cook the onions for a few minutes. Add the flour and cook for another minute. Stir in the milk and stock or water, bring to the boil, season and simmer gently for about 5 minutes. Grate the cheese, toss it into the soup and simmer until melted. *Do not allow to boil.*

Facing page: Cock-a-leekie

Hotch Potch

Known also as Hairst Bree (harvest broth), the flavour of this soup depends on the use of really fresh vegetables. The quaint name is thought to be a corruption of the French *hocher*, which means to shake together or mix up ingredients. Spring onions are sometimes called syboes in Scotland, from the French *cibo*.

Serves 6–8

1½ lb middle neck of lamb, chopped

8 oz shelled peas (1½ cups)

4 oz prepared broad beans (⅔ cup)

6 spring onions, trimmed and chopped

2 carrots, peeled and chopped

¾ lb turnip, peeled and chopped

1 medium cauliflower

1 small lettuce

salt

4 pints water (10 cups)

1 level tablespoon chopped parsley

Trim the meat and put it into a pan with the water and some salt. Bring the liquid to the boil then skim the surface carefully. Add half the peas and all the broad beans, onions, carrots and turnips and simmer the mixture for 1 hour.

Meanwhile trim the cauliflower and break it into small florets and finely shred the lettuce. When the hour is up add the rest of the peas, the cauliflower florets and the shredded lettuce and simmer the mixture for a further 30 minutes.

Check for seasoning then stir in the parsley and serve the soup in a heated tureen.

Scotch Broth

Often the meat in this most famous of broths would be removed, kept warm and served as the main course with caper or nasturtium seed sauce. Alternatively it would be cut into small pieces, returned to the broth and served as a main course in itself, accompanied by boiled potatoes or hodgils – oatmeal dumplings which can be cooked in the liquid (see page 61).

Serves 6–8

1 lb scrag end neck of lamb

3 pints water (7½ cups)

1 oz pearl barley (2 tablespoons)

2 oz dried peas, soaked overnight (4 tablespoons)

1 large carrot, sliced

1 large onion, sliced

1 small leek, trimmed and sliced

1 small turnip, diced

4 oz shredded cabbage

1 level tablespoon chopped parsley

Trim away the excess fat then put the lamb into a large pan with the water, pearl barley and peas and plenty of seasoning. Bring the liquid to the boil, cover the pan and simmer for 1 hour.

Add the prepared carrots, onion, leek and turnip, and when the broth returns to the boil simmer it for another 30 minutes. Stir in the cabbage and cook for a further 15 minutes. Skim off the fat, season to taste, stir in the parsley and serve piping hot.

Left: Roast Beef

Cock-a-Leekie

Serves 6–8

1 boiling fowl

1 bay leaf

1 lb leeks, slit, cleaned and cut into 1-inch pieces

4 pints stock or water (10 cups)

1 oz long grain rice (2 tablespoons)

4 oz dried prunes, soaked overnight (⅔ cup)

salt and pepper

Splendid copper pans in the kitchen of the Georgian House, 7 Charlotte Square, Edinburgh

This famous Scottish soup can often be found on the menu at a Burns Supper or St Andrew's Night Dinner. The addition of prunes to the soup was going out of vogue according to Meg Dod's recipe, and that was in 1826!

Put the bird and giblets into a large pan with the stock or water, add the bay leaf, leeks and plenty of seasoning. Bring the soup to the boil then skim the surface, reduce the heat, cover the pan and simmer for 2–3 hours, or until the bird is tender.

Remove the bird, giblets and bayleaf and skim off any fat from the surface. Add the rice and the prunes, drained, and simmer the soup for a further 30 minutes. Check for seasoning, then serve. Use the chicken, coated with a caper or egg sauce, as another course.

Kipper Pâté

This appetizing pâté makes an excellent light lunch or first course to a dinner party. If you do not have a blender pass the cooked fish through the finest disc on the mincer and then beat in the other ingredients with a spoon.

8 oz kippers
1 level teaspoon anchovy essence
3 oz melted butter (6 tablespoons)
salt and pepper
1 tablespoon single cream
¼ level teaspoon ground nutmeg

Put the kippers into a pan of cold water. Slowly bring them to the boil, simmer for one minute, then drain and remove all the bones and skin.

Put the pieces of fish into a liquidizer with the anchovy essence, 2 oz (¼ cup) of the melted butter, the cream, nutmeg and seasoning. Blend all these ingredients together to make a smooth consistency. Check for seasoning then turn into a small dish, smooth over the surface and pour the rest of the butter on top to form a seal.

Serve the pâté with fresh toast.

Fried Whiting

Traditionally whole whiting are fried clasping their tails in their mouths. To ensure they remain in that position during cooking fix each in place with a cocktail stick. This can easily be removed once the fish is cooked.

Serves 4
4 skinned whiting
1 large egg (size 2), beaten
dry white breadcrumbs
deep fat for frying

Fix the tails in position. Brush each fish with egg and toss it in the crumbs. Coat the fish a second time to ensure a really good surface.

Heat the deep fat – it is ready when a piece of bread turns brown in it after a minute. Lay the fish in the deep fat basket and gently lower them in to be cooked. They will take about 4 minutes.

Drain well then serve garnished with lemon wedges.

Fried Flukies

These fish are also sometimes known as flounders. Allow one per person and ask the fishmonger to clean it for you.

Melt about 2 oz ($\frac{1}{4}$ cup) butter and 2 tablespoons oil in a frying pan. Dip both sides of the fish in flour, seasoned with salt and pepper, and fry for 10–15 minutes or until golden brown. Turn the fish half way through the cooking time so they cook evenly. Drain on absorbent paper and serve garnished with lemon wedges and fried parsley sprigs.

Cod with Mustard Sauce

4 cod cutlets
$\frac{1}{2}$ pint milk (1$\frac{1}{4}$ cups)
$\frac{1}{2}$ pint water (1$\frac{1}{4}$ cups)
1 bay leaf
4 sprigs parsley
6 peppercorns
salt

For the sauce
1$\frac{1}{2}$ oz butter (3 tablespoons)
1$\frac{1}{4}$ oz plain flour (6 tablespoons)
1 rounded teaspoon made mustard
1 tablespoon vinegar

Mustard sauce is also a very tasty accompaniment to grilled herring or mackerel.

Wash the fish and put it into a shallow pan with a sprig of parsley under each cutlet to stop it from sticking to the pan. Pour in the milk and water and add the bay leaf, peppercorns and salt. Bring the liquid to the boil slowly then poach the fish for about 10 minutes or until cooked. Drain the cutlets well then place them in a dish to keep warm. Measure $\frac{3}{4}$ pint (scant 2 cups) of liquid from the pan. Melt the butter and stir in the flour. Remove from the heat and gradually blend in the strained $\frac{3}{4}$ pint fish liquor. When the sauce is smooth return the pan to the heat and bring the sauce to the boil to thicken, stirring all the time. Stir in the mustard and vinegar and check the sauce for other seasoning, then carefully spoon it over the fish and garnish the dish with parsley before serving. Often this recipe is accompanied by Clapshot (see page 70).

Fish Cakes with Egg Sauce

Makes 6

For the fish cakes

1 lb haddock or cod fillet

1 lb potatoes, cooked and creamed

6 peppercorns

1 bay leaf

4 cloves

a small piece of carrot and onion

1 level tablespoon chopped parsley

salt and pepper

1 large egg (size 2), well beaten

dried breadcrumbs

fat for deep frying

For the sauce

about ½ pint milk (1¼ cups)

1 oz plain flour (¼ cup)

1 oz margarine (2 tablespoons)

2 large eggs (size 2), hard boiled, shelled and chopped

Wipe the fish, put it into a pan with the peppercorns, bay leaf, cloves, carrot and onion, cover the fish with water and slowly bring the liquid to the boil. Reduce the heat, cover the pan and simmer the fish for about 10 minutes until cooked. Drain the fillets, reserving the liquor, then remove the skin and separate the fish into flakes.

Stir the fish into the potatoes with the parsley and check the mixture for seasoning. Divide it into six and, using a little seasoned flour, shape each piece into a fish cake about 3 inches in diameter. Put the beaten egg and the breadcrumbs onto separate plates, then coat each cake first with the egg and then with the crumbs.

Heat the fat in a deep fat fryer to 375°F/190°C (that is when a piece of bread browns in the fat in a minute) and cook the fish cakes three at a time for about 10 minutes until golden brown. Drain and serve with potato chips.

Melt the margarine, add the flour, then gradually blend in the fish liquid made up to ¾ pint (scant 2 cups) with milk to make a smooth sauce. Stirring all the time, bring the sauce to the boil and cook it for a minute to thicken. Stir in the egg and check the sauce for seasoning before pouring it into a sauce boat to serve with the fish cakes.

Cabbie Claw

Serves 4

1½ lb cod fillets

1 dessertspoon grated horseradish (2 teaspoons)

sprig of parsley

2 lb potatoes, boiled and mashed

1 hard boiled egg, roughly chopped

paprika

1 tablespoon chopped parsley

For the sauce

1½ oz flour (6 tablespoons)

1½ oz butter (3 tablespoons)

¾ pint fish liquor (2 cups) (see recipe)

salt and pepper

Place the cod fillets in a pan with the horseradish, sprig of parsley and salt. Cover with 1½ pints water, bring to the boil and simmer until the fish is cooked. Drain, reserving ¾ pint of the liquid for the sauce. Pipe a border of mashed potato around a large ashet and arrange the fish in the centre. Keep warm while making the sauce. Melt the butter in a saucepan, add the flour and cook for a few minutes without colouring. Add the fish liquid and milk, bring to the boil and cook to thicken. Stir in the hard boiled egg. season and pour over the fish. Garnish with parsley and paprika.

Grilled Mackerel with Gooseberry Sauce

For the sauce

½ lb fresh gooseberries

½ oz butter (1 tablespoon)

1 oz sugar (2 tablespoons)

a pinch of ground nutmeg

a little lemon juice

salt and pepper

Gooseberries are a native fruit of Scotland and the sharp flavour of this sauce is a wonderful accompaniment to the oily texture of the mackerel.

Allow one medium fish per person. Gut and wash the mackerel or ask the fishmonger to do it for you. Make three diagonal scores through the thick part on either side of the fish using a sharp knife. Brush them with a little melted butter and sprinkle them with salt and pepper. Cook the mackerel on a buttered grill pan under a rather slow grill. They will take about 20 minutes in all and are best brushed once or twice with butter as they are turned. Serve with the gooseberry sauce.

Wash the gooseberries – there is no need to prepare them. Place the fruit in a pan and cook it to a soft pulp with the butter. Rub the fruit through a sieve, then stir in the sugar, salt and pepper and the lemon juice before serving. A teaspoon of chopped chives can be added to the sauce also.

Stuffed Baked Mackerel

Serves 4

4 small mackerel, heads removed and cleaned by the fishmonger

2 eggs, hard boiled, shelled and chopped

3 oz Scottish Cheddar cheese, grated (¾ cup)

½ level teaspoon dry mustard

1 oz butter, melted (2 tablespoons)

1 level tablespoon chopped parsley

1 lemon

Wipe the mackerel and make three deep incisions on each side about half an inch apart.

Mix the finely chopped eggs with the cheese, mustard, butter and parsley, the juice and grated rind of half the lemon, and plenty of seasoning. When the ingredients are well blended divide the stuffing between the fish, packing it into the cavities left after they were cleaned.

Put the fish into a lightly buttered shallow dish and cover with foil. Bake at Gas 6/400°F/200°C for about 40 minutes or until cooked. Garnish with the other half of the lemon cut into slices.

Soused or Pickled Herrings

Remove the fins and tail from each herring using a pair of scissors, then cut the fish open along the underside from head to tail. Lay the fish flat on a board, skin side upwards. Press down firmly all the way along the backbone, then ease out the bone with the help of a knife.

Lay the fillets of fish on a flat surface and scatter each with a few rings of onion, then roll them up tightly. Lay the rolls in the dish, packing them closely together so they do not unroll. Scatter the rest of the onion rings on top, add the bay leaf, peppercorns and allspice berries and the whole chilli. Pour over the vinegar and water. Cover the dish with foil and cook the herrings at Gas 3/325°F/160°C for 1 hour.

Leave the herrings overnight to cool in their liquor. Serve the dish with thinly sliced bread and butter.

Serves 6

6 small herrings, cleaned by the fishmonger

1 medium onion, peeled and thinly sliced

1 bay leaf

6 peppercorns

3 allspice berries

1 whole chilli

$\frac{1}{4}$ pint vinegar ($\frac{2}{3}$ cup)

$\frac{1}{4}$ pint cold water ($\frac{2}{3}$ cup)

Boiled Beef with Hodgils

Soak the beef overnight in cold water. Weigh the joint and calculate the cooking time at 25 minutes to the pound plus 25 minutes.

Put the beef into a pan with the bay leaf, cover the meat with cold water and slowly bring it to the boil. Cover the pan and simmer for the calculated cooking time, starting from when it reaches the boil. Add the prepared vegetables $1\frac{1}{2}$ hours before the beef is ready.

Mix the oatmeal with the chives and plenty of seasoning. Using the fat from the top of the liquid in which the beef is cooking, bind the oatmeal mixture together, then roll it into balls making about ten in all. Leave the hodgils to stand for 20 minutes, then cook them in with the meat for 15 minutes.

To serve, lift the meat onto an ashet and surround it with the hodgils and vegetables. The liquid in which the meat was cooked can be served as gravy but check it first for seasoning.

Serves 6

3–4 lb salt beef

1 bay leaf

$1\frac{1}{2}$ lb carrots, peeled and quartered

1 lb onions, peeled

$\frac{3}{4}$ lb parsnips or swede, peeled and cut into large cubes

For the hodgils

8 oz oatmeal ($1\frac{1}{3}$ cups)

1 tablespoon chopped chives

salt and pepper

Prosen Hot Pot

Serves 8

3 lb neck or shoulder of mutton

1 lb onions, sliced

2 lb carrots, sliced

1 lb tomatoes, skinned and sliced

white stock

salt and pepper

This recipe comes from the Pennan Inn at Pennan in Grampian. Pennan is a lovely, unspoilt fishing village on the Moray Firth, and the Inn is run by Myra and Les Rose. This is a tasty and economical recipe for a lamb hot pot.

Trim chops, removing sinew and spinal cord. Arrange in layers in an ovenproof dish the chops, carrots, tomatoes and onions, seasoning each layer. Add enough stock to come half way up the meat. Cover and bake for $2-2\frac{1}{2}$ hours at Gas 4/350°F/180°C.

Boiled Mutton with Caper Sauce

1 leg of mutton 6–7 lb

4 large onions

$1\frac{1}{2}$ lb carrots, peeled and chunked

1 parsnip, peeled and chunked

8 peppercorns

2 bay leaves

salt

For the sauce

2 oz margarine ($\frac{1}{4}$ cup)

2 oz plain flour ($\frac{1}{2}$ cup)

$\frac{1}{2}$ pint milk ($1\frac{1}{4}$ cups)

$\frac{1}{2}$ pint meat stock, taken from the mutton ($1\frac{1}{4}$ cups)

2 oz capers ($\frac{1}{3}$ cup)

Calculate the cooking time at 25 minutes per pound plus 25 minutes. Put the joint into a large pan, cover with cold water, add the peppercorns, bay leaves and salt, and bring the liquid slowly to the boil. Calculate the cooking time from when the liquid boils. Cover the pan and simmer for the required time adding the vegetables after 1 hour.

When it is cooked lift the joint onto a large ashet, coat with the caper sauce and surround with the vegetables.

To make the caper sauce

Melt the margarine, add the flour and when well blended gradually stir in the milk and stock to make a smooth sauce. Bring the sauce to the boil to thicken, stirring constantly, then add the capers and check for seasoning.

Pour about half the sauce over the joint and serve the rest separately.

Howtowdie with Drappit Eggs

This early nineteenth century dish has a very strong French influence. Howtowdie comes from the Old French *hutaudeau*, meaning a pullet. Drappit eggs are poached eggs; they look pretty surrounding the chicken on their nest of spinach and this is an excellent way of stretching a small chicken to feed six.

Serves 6

3 lb roasting chicken

For the stuffing

3 oz breadcrumbs ($\frac{1}{2}$ cup)

1 small onion, peeled and chopped

$\frac{1}{2}$ level teaspoon dried herbs

a pinch of paprika pepper

2 oz ham, chopped ($\frac{1}{3}$ cup)

2 oz melted butter ($\frac{1}{4}$ cup)

To complete the dish

4 oz butter ($\frac{1}{2}$ cup)

8 button onions or 2 large onions, peeled and sliced

6 peppercorns

3 cloves

3 allspice berries

$\frac{1}{2}$ pint chicken stock ($1\frac{1}{4}$ cups)

salt

6 standard eggs (size 3)

2 lb spinach

Wipe the chicken inside and out and reserve the liver for later. Mix the breadcrumbs with the onion for the stuffing, together with the herbs, pepper and ham. Bind the ingredients together with the butter then place the stuffing into the bird and truss it.

In a large flameproof pan melt the 4 ounces ($\frac{1}{2}$ cup) of butter. Add the chicken and onions and brown them over a medium heat. Add the peppercorns, cloves, allspice berries, stock and salt, and bring the liquid to the boil. Cover the dish and cook in a moderate oven (Gas 4/350°F/180°C) for 1–1$\frac{1}{4}$ hours or until the bird is tender.

Meanwhile prepare and cook the spinach, purée it and beat in a little thick cream and extra butter.

When the chicken is cooked strain the stock into a pan, add the liver and poach it for about 3 minutes until cooked. Leave it on one side. Poach the eggs in the stock then arrange nests of spinach around the edge of a large ashet. Place an egg in the centre of each with the cooked chicken in the centre of the dish.

Rub the liver through a sieve into the stock to thicken it. Pour some of it over the chicken and serve the rest separately.

Pigeon Casserole

During the last century most town houses had a dovecot and pigeons were a useful extra source of meat. They are still plentiful, though rather neglected, and with long slow cooking they make an excellent casserole.

Serves 4

2 pigeons

1 tablespoon cooking oil

1 oz butter (2 tablespoons)

¼ lb streaky bacon rashers

½ lb onion, peeled and sliced

bouquet garni – bought or made from a bay leaf, parsley stalk, blade of mace and sprig of thyme tied together with string

½ pint tomato juice (1¼ cups)

½ pint chicken stock (1¼ cups)

2 slices white bread

a little lard

Wipe the pigeons, then cut each one in half along the breast and back bone.

Heat the butter and oil together, add the pigeon halves and over a high heat brown them quickly. Transfer to a casserole dish.

Cut the rind and any bones from the bacon, then cut each rasher into pieces and fry together with the onion in the fat left in the pan. When they start to brown transfer both ingredients to the casserole dish.

Pour over the tomato juice and stock, add the bouquet garni, then check the sauce for seasoning. Cover the casserole and bake the dish at Gas 5/375°F/190°C for about 2 hours or until the meat is tender.

Just before the casserole is cooked cut the crusts off the bread and cut each slice into four triangles. Heat the lard in a frying pan and fry the pieces of bread until they are golden brown on each side.

When the pigeon casserole is ready, remove it from the oven, take out the bouquet garni and scatter the triangles of bread over the surface.

Serve with buttered carrots, creamed tatties and peas.

Mince Collops

This is a good Scottish family dish sometimes referred to as Scotch Collops. Collop is probably derived from the French *escalope*, small slivers of meat.

Serves 4

1 lb best quality minced beef (2 cups, firmly packed)

1 medium onion, peeled and sliced

salt

1 tablespoon mushroom ketchup

½ pint beef stock (1¼ cups)

1 level tablespoon oatmeal

½ oz dripping (1 tablespoon)

Melt the dripping in a pan, add the onion and fry it for a few minutes, then stir in the mince and brown it carefully, stirring constantly to avoid lumps. Mix in the salt and stock with the mushroom ketchup and oatmeal. Simmer for about 45 minutes or until the meat is cooked.

Serve on a large ashet garnished with sippets of toast or a border of mashed potatoes.

Forfar Bridies

These individual pies from the town north of Dundee were mentioned by J. M. Barrie in his famous book *Sentimental Tommy*. The pastry in those days was made simply from flour and water, but as you will see the modern Forfar Bridies are made with a shortcrust dough. Once cooked they are very similar to Cornish Pasties.

Makes 4

For the pastry

1 lb plain flour (3½–4 cups)

a pinch of salt

4 oz margarine (½ cup)

4 oz lard (½ cup)

For the filling

1 lb chuck steak

3 oz prepared shredded suet (⅔ cup)

1 onion, peeled and finely chopped

Sift the flour and salt together into a bowl, add the fats cut into small pieces and rub them in until evenly distributed. Stir in sufficient cold water to make a fairly stiff dough then turn it onto a floured surface and knead gently. Divide the dough into four.

Trim the steak, removing any excess fat, then pound it with a meat hammer or rolling pin. Cut the meat into thin strips and mix it with the suet and onion and plenty of seasoning.

Roll each piece of dough out to a 7-inch round or an oval. Divide the filling between them and seal the edges well with water, scalloping the edges with the fingers and a thumb.

Make a hole in the centre of each with a skewer and bake at Gas 6/400°F/200°C for 20 minutes. Reduce the temperature to Gas 4/350°F/180°C and bake for a further 35–45 minutes or until golden brown.

Serve hot.

Kingdom of Fife Pie

Although pork is not popular in traditional Scottish cookery and has been particularly spurned in the Highlands, pigs are kept on the border areas and a number of recipes survive from the days when pickling was a necessary form of preservation. If you can get it, it is particularly good in this rabbit pie.

Serves 4–6

For the pastry

10 oz plain flour (2½ cups)

4 oz margarine (½ cup)

4 oz lard (½ cup)

For the filling

1–1½ lb rabbit, jointed

8 oz pickled pork or green cured bacon

2 hard boiled eggs, quartered

½ pint stock (1¼ cups)

For the stuffing balls

3 oz fresh breadcrumbs (½ cup)

1 oz fat bacon, chopped (2 tablespoons)

a pinch of dried thyme

1 egg

salt and pepper

Sieve the flour and a pinch of salt into a mixing bowl. Add the fats cut into 1-inch pieces and mix them in, then stir in sufficient cold water to make a soft dough. Turn the dough onto a floured surface and roll it into an oblong, then fold the top third over the middle third and the bottom third up over the other two thirds. Seal the edges, turn the dough a ¼ turn, re-roll and fold the pastry once more. Then leave the dough in a cool place for 15 minutes to rest before repeating the whole process twice more.

While the pastry is resting prepare the filling. Keep the liver from the rabbit on one side, place the joints in a 3-pint pie dish with the pickled pork, cut into pieces, and the quartered hard boiled eggs.

Mix the breadcrumbs with the bacon, thyme and seasoning. Add the rabbit liver finely chopped, then bind the mixture together with the egg. Divide the stuffing into eight and roll each piece into a ball. Place the balls of stuffing in the pie amongst the other ingredients and pour in the stock.

Cover the pie with the pastry, decorate it, and glaze the pastry with beaten egg. Bake at Gas 7/425°F/220°C for 15 minutes, then reduce the heat to Gas 3/325°F/160°C and bake for a further 1¼ hours or until golden brown and cooked.

Serve hot or cold.

Giblet Pie

This pie is traditionally served during the Christmas holidays.

Serves 3–4

cooked turkey giblets

1 lb thinly cut stewing steak

1 oz plain flour seasoned with salt and pepper ($\frac{1}{4}$ cup)

1 bay leaf

about $\frac{1}{4}$ pint giblet stock ($\frac{2}{3}$ cup)

1 7-oz packet puff pastry, thawed

a little beaten egg for glaze

Remove all the meat from the neck and chop it with the liver, heart and kidney. Cut the beef into pieces and toss it in the flour. Mix the beef with the chopped giblets and put them into a 1–1$\frac{1}{2}$ pint pie dish. Add the bay leaf and pour in enough stock to come just over half way up the sides of the dish. Cover the pie with the pastry and decorate it with a fluted edge. Make a hole in the centre to release the steam then brush the pastry with egg glaze.

Bake the pie at Gas 7/425°F/220°C for 15 minutes. Reduce the heat to Gas 3/325°F/160°C and cook for a further 1$\frac{1}{4}$ hours or until the pastry is golden brown and the meat tender.

Serve piping hot with creamed potatoes and buttered cabbage.

Inky Pinky

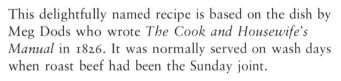

This delightfully named recipe is based on the dish by Meg Dods who wrote *The Cook and Housewife's Manual* in 1826. It was normally served on wash days when roast beef had been the Sunday joint.

Cut the cold beef into slices, allowing about 2 rounds per person. Remove any skin or fat. Add 2 sliced and boiled carrots per person.

Place the beef and the carrots in $\frac{1}{2}$ pint (1$\frac{1}{4}$ cups) well flavoured gravy and simmer them slowly so they are really heated. Stir a dessertspoonful (2 teaspoons) of vinegar and salt and pepper into the gravy. Blend 2 teaspoonsfuls of cornflour to a smooth paste with water and mix in a little of the hot gravy. Return it to the main dish and cook until it thickens.

Serve Inky Pinky hot with sippets of toast.

Rabbit Dumpling

Try this tasty steamed rabbit pudding as a change from steak and kidney pudding on a cold winter day.

Sift the flour for the pastry and a pinch of salt into a bowl. Stir in the suet then bind the ingredients together with enough cold water to make a fairly soft dough. Cut a quarter off to use later for the lid then roll the rest out into a round and line a 2-pint pudding basin, lightly greased, making sure it comes just above the rim of the bowl. Using a sharp knife, cut the meat from the rabbit and cut it into small pieces. Toss the meat in the seasoned flour, then mix in the grated carrot, bacon and onion. When all the ingredients are well combined, turn the filling into the lined basin. Add the stock. Roll the remaining piece of pastry for the lid into a circle the size of the basin, moisten the edges, then lift it into place, sealing the edges really well together. Snip off any excess dough with a pair of scissors.

Cover the dumpling with a piece of foil, making a pleat down the centre to allow the dumpling to rise. Fasten it in place with string and make a string handle across the top so the basin can be easily lifted.

Steam the dumpling either over a pan of simmering water or standing in water that comes halfway up the sides of the basin – it should cook in about $2\frac{1}{2}$ hours. Replenish the pan with more boiling water when necessary.

Serve the pudding straight from the bowl or turn it out onto a plate. Complete the meal with curley kail.

Serves 4

For the pastry

8 oz self-raising flour (2 cups)

a pinch of salt

3 oz prepared shredded suet ($\frac{2}{3}$ cup)

For the filling

1 rabbit

$\frac{1}{2}$ lb onion, peeled and finely chopped

$\frac{1}{2}$ lb carrots, peeled and grated

4 oz streaky bacon, chopped

1 oz plain flour, seasoned ($\frac{1}{4}$ cup)

4 tablespoons chicken stock ($\frac{1}{4}$ cup)

Stovies

Melt the dripping in a large pan, add a layer of sliced potatoes, then a layer of onion and next a layer of meat. Add enough stock or water to cover then repeat the layers once again and season the dish thoroughly.

Cover and cook over a moderate heat, shaking the pan occasionally, for about 30 minutes or until the potatoes are tender and the liquid is absorbed.

Serve with cold meats.

Serves 4

4 oz cold, diced lamb ($\frac{2}{3}$ cup)

$1\frac{1}{2}$ lb potatoes, peeled and thinly sliced

1 large onion, sliced

1 level tablespoon dripping

stock or water

salt and pepper

Potted Hough

Potting is one of the oldest ways of preserving food. The potting of fish and game was popular in Scotland in the eighteenth and nineteenth centuries as it was a convenient method of sending food to friends and relatives. Today potted fish, game and other meats makes a pleasant starter to a meal. This is also a very tasty and convenient savoury dish for a picnic.

Serves 4

1 lb hough (shin of beef)

a 2-lb beef shin bone or knuckle of veal

1 level teaspoon salt

6 allspice berries

6 peppercorns

1 small bay leaf

Put the meat and bone into a pan and cover with cold water – about 3 pints ($7\frac{1}{2}$ cups). Bring to the boil, reduce the heat and simmer for about 3 hours until the meat is really tender.

Cut the meat into small pieces or mince it to make a smoother texture, and remove any meat from the bone. Return the bone to the pan, add the salt, allspice berries, peppercorns and bay leaf and boil the liquid rapidly until it has reduced by about half. Put the meat into one large or two small moulds, pour in the stock and leave to set. Next day unmould the potted hough and serve with a salad.

Scotch Eggs

Makes 5

1 lb sausagemeat (2 cups, firmly packed)

5 hard boiled eggs, shelled

1 large egg (size 2), beaten

a dusting of flour

dry white breadcrumbs

deep fat for frying

Dust each egg with a little flour. Divide the sausagemeat into five and on a floured surface work each piece into an oval. Place an egg in the centre of each one and mould the sausagemeat round it, making sure the surface is free from cracks. Put the beaten egg and breadcrumbs onto separate plates and coat each egg first in the liquid egg and then in the breadcrumbs so that the surface is completely covered. Coat each egg again if you like to ensure a really good surface.

Heat a deep fat fryer half full of oil to 360°F/185°C, lower in the eggs and cook them for about 5–6 minutes. If the fat is too hot the outside will brown before the sausagemeat is cooked. Drain when cooked and leave to cool.

Serve with a salad for lunch or as a picnic food.

Facing page: Tea table laid with Selkirk Bannock, Dundee Cake, Drop Scones, Black Bun and Shortbread

There are many marvellous vegetable dishes to be found in Scotland, the most famous of them being Tatties-an'-Neeps (mashed potatoes and turnips), traditionally served with Haggis. But here are a few more that you will, I know, find delicious.

Clapshot

This is a dish from the Orkney Islands.

Serves 4–6
1 lb potatoes, peeled
1 lb turnips
1–2 oz dripping (2–4 tablespoons)
1 level tablespoon chopped chives
salt and pepper

Cook and mash the potatoes, and cook and mash the turnips. Beat the two vegetables together.

Stir in dripping to taste and the chives, then check the mixture for seasoning.

Beat the clapshot over the heat until well mixed then serve piping hot. This dish is sometimes served with haggis.

Colcannon

This is the Highlanders' version of this delicious vegetable accompaniment to meat, a rather sophisticated bubble and squeak. It derives from Kailcannon, a recipe thought to have been brought from Ireland with the potato in the eighteenth century. In other regions the carrot and turnip are omitted.

Serves 4–6
1 lb potatoes, cooked and creamed
1 lb cabbage
½ lb carrots, peeled
½ lb turnips, peeled
2 oz butter (¼ cup)
1 tablespoon brown sauce
salt and pepper

Wash and shred the cabbage, removing all the thick stems, and cook it in boiling salted water for about 15 minutes or until tender. Chop and cook the carrots and turnips together until tender, then mash them until smooth.

Melt the butter in a pan, add the creamed potatoes, cabbage, and carrot and turnip purée. Stir all these ingredients together until they are thoroughly heated, then mix in the brown sauce and check the dish for seasoning before serving. Colcannon is specially good with cold lamb.

Kailkenny

Serves 3–4

1 lb potatoes, cooked and creamed

1 lb cabbage, shredded and cooked

salt and pepper

4 tablespoons single cream

This vegetable dish is from the east of Scotland and is a variation of Colcannon.

Mix the creamed potatoes and cooked cabbage together then moisten the mixture with the cream and season it well.

Rumbledethumps

Serves 3–4

1 lb potatoes, cooked and creamed

1 lb cabbage, shredded and cooked

salt and pepper

2 oz butter ($\frac{1}{4}$ cup)

1 tablespoon chopped chives or 4 spring onions, chopped

Yet another version of Colcannon, this time from the Border. This one is just as good as the others.

Mix the creamed potatoes and cooked cabbage together, beat in the butter and when it has melted stir in the chives or onions with plenty of seasoning to taste.

Skirlie

Serves 3–4

2 oz dripping ($\frac{1}{4}$ cup)

1 large onion, peeled and finely chopped

about 4 oz oatmeal ($\frac{2}{3}$ cup)

salt and pepper

This can be served on its own with chappit (mashed) potatoes, and is also an accompaniment to roast pheasant or grouse.

Melt the dripping, add the onion and fry it slowly, stirring occasionally until evenly brown. Stir in enough oatmeal to absorb the fat, add seasoning and cook for about 10–15 minutes until thoroughly cooked.

Serve with chappit (mashed) potatoes.

Left: Typsy Laird

Apple Frushie

Serves 6

For the pastry

10 oz plain flour (2¼ cups)

a pinch of salt

2 oz lard (¼ cup)

3 oz margarine (6 tablespoons)

1 egg yolk

For the filling

1 lb cooking apples, peeled and sliced

2 oz caster sugar (¼ cup)

Frushie is an old Scots word meaning brittle or crumbly and it obviously refers to the pastry in this tart. This is a popular pudding in the west of Scotland and is normally eaten with cream.

Sift the flour and salt for the pastry into a bowl, add the fats and rub them in until evenly distributed. Bind the ingredients together with the egg yolk and enough cold water to make a fairly stiff dough. Turn the dough onto a floured surface and knead it lightly. Then, using half of the pastry, line the base of an 8-inch pie plate, letting it overlap the edges by half an inch. Layer the apples and sugar into the centre.

Roll the remaining piece of dough into a round a little larger than the plate and cut it into half-inch strips. Closely trellis the top of the pie with the pastry so that the filling is almost enclosed. Stick the strips to the sides with water. Overlap the extra pastry to form a thick edge and flute it for decoration.

Brush the pastry with milk then bake the tart at Gas 5/375°F/190°C for 40 minutes or until golden brown.

Scottish Plum Crumble

Serves 4

1½ lb ripe plums

2–3 oz soft brown sugar (¼ cup, firmly packed)

1 tablespoon water

For the crumble

4 oz plain flour (1 cup)

2 oz rolled oats (⅔ cup)

2 oz soft brown sugar (4 tablespoons, firmly packed)

½ level teaspoon ground cinnamon

3 oz butter (6 tablespoons)

Wash the plums, cut them in half and remove the stones. Mix the fruit with the sugar, turn it into a 1½–2 pint pie dish and pour over the water.

Sift the flour and cinnamon into a bowl, add the oats and rub in the butter until evenly distributed. Stir in the sugar then turn the crumble onto the plums and spread it to the sides so they are completely covered.

Bake the crumble at Gas 4/350°F/180°C for 45–50 minutes or until the topping is golden brown and the fruit cooked.

Serve hot with custard.

Apple and Cranberry Pie

Serves 4–6

For the pastry

8 oz plain flour (2 cups)

2 oz margarine ($\frac{1}{4}$ cup)

2 oz lard ($\frac{1}{4}$ cup)

For the filling

1$\frac{1}{2}$ lbs cooking apples

4 oz fresh cranberries (1 cup)

6–8 oz granulated sugar ($\frac{3}{4}$–1 cup)

The scarlet cranberries in this recipe make an extra special apple pie which looks and tastes wonderful as a winter pudding. If fresh cranberries are not available use an 8-ounce can of whole cranberry sauce and reduce the quantity of sugar.

Sift the flour and a pinch of salt into a bowl, add the fats cut into small pieces and then rub them in until evenly distributed. Stir in sufficient cold water to make a fairly stiff dough. Turn it onto a working surface and knead quickly until smooth, then wrap it in greaseproof paper and leave in a cool place while preparing the filling.

Peel, core and slice the apples. Pick over the cranberries then mix the two fruits together. Mix in the sugar and turn the filling into a 1$\frac{1}{2}$-pint pie dish.

Roll the pastry out to 1$\frac{1}{2}$ inches larger than the pie dish, cut a 1-inch wide strip from around the edge and lay it onto the rim of the pie dish, sticking it into position with a little water. Lift the main piece of pastry into place again, sticking the edges well together with water. Trim off any excess dough then knock up the edges and mark them into small flutes with the back of a knife. Brush the pastry with water and sprinkle thickly with granulated sugar. Bake the pie at Gas 6/400°F/200°C for 20 minutes. Reduce the heat to Gas 4/350°F/180°C for a further 30 minutes or until the fruit is soft.

Serve with custard.

Blaeberry Pie

Blaeberries are sometimes difficult to obtain unless you are lucky enough to live close to moorland where they grow wild. I have tested the recipe using blackcurrants and it is as good.

Serves 6–8

For the pastry

12 oz self-raising flour (3 cups)

½ level teaspoon baking powder

6 oz lard (¾ cup)

For the filling and glaze

12 oz blaeberries (3 cups)

3 oz soft brown sugar (⅓ cup, firmly packed)

1 level teaspoon plain flour

a little milk

a little caster sugar

Sift the flour and baking powder and a pinch of salt into a bowl. Rub in the lard then bind the mixture together with cold water to make a dough a little shorter than short crust pastry.

Using half the pastry line a 9-inch ovenproof plate. Mix the blaeberries with the soft brown sugar and teaspoon of plain flour and turn them onto the lined plate. Roll out the remaining dough to a circle just a little larger than the plate. Moisten the edge of the pastry and lift the lid into place, sealing the edges really well. Mark the edges with a fork, brush the surface with milk and sprinkle over caster sugar.

Bake the pie at Gas 6/400°F/200°C for about 30 minutes until golden brown. Serve warm with custard.

Lemon Pudding

This delicious old recipe should be served cold with switched (whipped) cream. The filling is similar to a very luscious lemon curd.

Serves 6–8

1 14-oz packet puff pastry, thawed

For the filling

3 standard eggs (size 3)

3 egg yolks

6 oz melted butter (¾ cup)

8 oz caster sugar (1 cup)

2 lemons

Line a 10-inch, deep pie plate with the pastry and decorate the edge. Bake the case blind at Gas 7/425°F/220°C for 20–25 minutes, removing the paper and baking beans for the last 10 minutes.

Beat the eggs, egg yolks and sugar together, mix in the melted butter with the rind of one lemon and juice of both. Pour the mixture into the pastry case and bake the pudding at Gas 4/350°F/180°C for about 30–40 minutes until it is golden brown (the filling will still be quite soft at this stage).

Leave to cool and set, then serve sliced.

Butterscotch Meringue Flan

Serves 4–6

For the flan case

2 oz butter, softened ($\frac{1}{4}$ cup)

2 oz icing sugar, sifted ($\frac{1}{2}$ cup)

1 standard egg (size 4)

6 oz plain flour ($1\frac{1}{2}$ cups)

For the filling

2 oz butter ($\frac{1}{4}$ cup)

4 oz dark soft brown sugar ($\frac{1}{2}$ cup, firmly packed)

1 oz cornflour ($\frac{1}{4}$ cup)

$\frac{1}{2}$ pint milk ($1\frac{1}{4}$ cups)

2 large eggs (size 2), separated

4 oz caster sugar ($\frac{1}{2}$ cup)

an 8-inch fluted flan ring

This pretty flan is not expensive to make but is quite delicious with its creamy, butterscotch-flavoured filling and lightly browned meringue topping.

Beat the butter and icing sugar together for the pastry, until light and fluffy in colour and texture. Beat the egg, then add it gradually to the cream mixture, beating well between each addition. Sift the flour and mix it into the other ingredients to form a fairly soft dough. Wrap the pastry in greaseproof paper and leave it in a cool place for about 15 minutes to rest.

Stand the flan ring on a baking tray and grease them both. Roll the pastry into a circle 2 inches (5 cm) larger than the flan ring. Fold it in three, then lift it into the flan ring, open it out and ease the pastry over the base and up the sides, pushing it well into the fluted edge. Trim off the excess dough and fill the centre of the flan case with a large piece of foil, crumpling it into the sides, and bake the pastry 'blind' at Gas 4/350°F/180°C for 20 minutes. Then remove the foil and continue baking the case for a further 5–10 minutes to brown. Remove the flan ring but leave the case on the baking tray.

Melt the butter and brown sugar together until both are dissolved. Blend the cornflour with a little of the milk to make a smooth paste, then pour the rest of the milk into the butter and soft brown sugar mixture and, when they have combined, pour a little of the liquid onto the cornflour. Blend it in, then pour this back into the main bulk of liquid.

Stirring all the time, bring the sauce to the boil to thicken, then add the egg yolks and cook the filling for a further minute. Pour it into the flan case.

Whisk the egg whites until they are stiff and stand in straight peaks, add 2 tablespoons from the caster sugar and re-whisk the meringue until it regains its original stiffness. Fold in the rest of the sugar lightly and quickly, then spoon it over the flan leaving the surface rough. Bake at Gas 6/400°F/200°C for 5–10 minutes until tinged golden brown.

Floating Islands

There are two versions of this recipe, one much richer than the other. Here is the simpler.

Whisk the egg whites with half the sugar until stiff enough to stand in straight peaks, then fold in the rest of the sugar.

Bring the milk to the boil then add the meringue in spoonfuls – there should be six in all – using a second spoon to release it from the first one. Poach the meringues in the simmering milk for about 5 minutes, turning them halfway through the cooking time. Lift them out when cooked onto a piece of kitchen paper to cool and drain.

Beat the egg yolks for the base with the vanilla essence, caster sugar and cornflour. Pour in a little of the hot milk and when the mixture is smooth return it to the rest of the milk and, stirring all the time, bring it to the boil.

Pour the custard into a serving dish, arrange the meringues on top and leave the pudding to cool.

When served it can be sprinkled with a little grated chocolate if liked.

Serves 4

2 egg whites (large, size 2)

2 oz caster sugar ($\frac{1}{4}$ cup)

For the custard base

1 pint milk (2$\frac{1}{2}$ cups)

2 oz caster sugar ($\frac{1}{4}$ cup)

2 egg yolks (large, size 2)

a little vanilla essence

2 level teaspoons cornflour

Queen of Puddings

Melt the butter in the milk, stir it into the breadcrumbs in a bowl, add 1 oz (2 tablespoons) of sugar and leave the mixture on one side to soak for 30 minutes. Stir the egg yolks into the soaked breadcrumb mixture, pour it into a 2-pint ovenproof dish and bake the base at Gas 4/350°F/180°C for 30 minutes or until just set.

Warm the jam and spread it over the cooked base. Whisk the egg whites until they are stiff and stand in straight peaks, add 2 tablespoonsfuls from the remaining sugar and whisk again, then fold in the rest of the sugar and turn the meringue onto the jam. Carefully spread it to the side leaving the surface rough.

Sprinkle the surface with a little extra caster sugar then bake at Gas 3/325°F/160°C for 10 minutes or until the meringue is tinged golden brown. Serve with single cream.

Serves 4–6

1 pint milk (2$\frac{1}{4}$ cups)

1 oz butter (2 tablespoons)

3 oz freshly made white breadcrumbs ($\frac{1}{2}$ cup)

3 oz caster sugar ($\frac{1}{3}$ cup)

the finely grated rind of 1 small orange

2 large eggs (size 2), separated

3 tablespoons raspberry jam

Gooseberry Batter Pudding

Serves 6

¾ pint milk (scant 2 cups)

3 large eggs (size 2)

2 oz plain flour (½ cup)

¼ level teaspoon ground nutmeg

4 oz caster sugar (½ cup)

¾ lb ripe gooseberries (3 cups)

sifted icing sugar

Grease liberally with butter a shallow ovenproof dish of 2 pints liquid capacity. Top and tail the gooseberries and put them into the dish.

Warm the milk to blood heat. Sieve the flour and nutmeg into a bowl, stir in the sugar, then break the eggs into the centre and with a wooden spoon gradually work the dry ingredients into the liquid, adding the milk as you work to make a smooth batter. Beat the batter for a minute to incorporate as much air as possible, then pour the batter into the dish. (The batter may be made in a blender if liked: put the eggs, sugar, nutmeg and flour into the goblet and when the mixture is smooth gradually add the milk.)

Bake the pudding at Gas 6/400°F/200°C for 45 minutes. If the surface is too brown after 30 minutes cover it with a sheet of greaseproof paper, then continue to bake the pudding for a further 15 minutes or until it is just firm.

Immediately the dessert is cooked sprinkle the surface thickly with icing sugar and serve with single cream.

Cloutie Dumpling

Serves 4

3 oz oatmeal (¼ cup)

3 oz plain flour (¾ cup)

3 oz prepared shredded suet (⅔ cup)

3 oz caster sugar (⅓ cup)

2 oz sultanas (¼ cup)

2 oz currants (¼ cup)

1 level teaspoon mixed spice

½ level teaspoon bicarbonate of soda

7½ fl oz milk (1 cup), soured with ½ teaspoon vinegar

This pudding takes its name from the cloth or clout in which it is boiled.

Mix all the dry ingredients together, then bind the mixture with the milk and vinegar.

Dip a pudding cloth in boiling water, then lay it in a pudding basin. Dredge the surface with flour, spoon in the mixture and draw up the cloth, leaving enough space for the pudding to swell. Tie the cloth with string. Place a saucer in the middle of a large pan filled with boiling water, lower in the dumpling, and simmer for 2½ hours, replenishing the water as required with more boiling water.

Turn the dumpling out of the cloth onto a plate, dredge with sugar and serve with custard.

Marmalade Pudding

This is a substantial pudding, ideal to serve on a cold winter's night.

Serves 6

8 oz fresh breadcrumbs (1½ cups)

3 oz prepared shredded suet (⅔ cup)

4 oz granulated sugar (½ cup)

3 standard eggs (size 3)

4 tablespoons milk

½ lb marmalade (¾ cup)

Mix the breadcrumbs with the suet and sugar, then bind the ingredients together with the eggs and milk.

Place 2 tablespoons of marmalade in the bottom of a greased 2-pint pudding basin. Turn the mixture onto it then cover the bowl with foil or greaseproof paper. Seal and bake the pudding at Gas 4/350°F/180°C for about 1 hour.

Serve piping hot with the rest of the marmalade melted to form a sauce.

Loch Lomond

The Meal of Ceremony

The Scottish tea has always been a meal of great
importance, a time when the family gathers together
around a table groaning with sweet breads and biscuits,
cakes and freshly-baked scones, dishes of jams and
jellies made with local berries, and perhaps eggs and
cold meats too – a proper, splendid, old-fashioned high
tea.

From its humble origins of bannocks cooked on a
bakestone over the peat fire, the Scottish housewife's
baking skills have developed this meal to a point of
unrivalled good fare. And yet tea in Scotland remains a
homely, family affair, the good plain food common to
castle or croft.

The teabread began to develop as a Scottish speciality
in the fifteenth century, and in Tudor times it was the
custom to add sweet ingredients – dried fruits, spices,
honey and butter – to the basic all-purpose biscuit
dough, making a rich, fruity loaf. From this evolved the
fancy cake, which has reached its peak of perfection in
the famous Dundee cake. These dried fruits and spices
were dear to import, however, and only the wealthier
citizens could afford them. Perhaps this is why so much
of the classic Scottish baking consists of the simplest of
recipes. What could be more delicious than the plainest
but lightest of scones or drop scones, the crunchiest of
shortbreads or oatcakes? The art of home baking
developed properly in the eighteenth century with the
introduction of the kitchen range with its integral oven.
Before this only the larger houses had their own ovens,
and breads were usually taken to the public bakehouses,
which tended to be in religious establishments. At the
beginning of the same century eggs began to be used as
raising agents, in seed cake, for example, and this was
the forerunner of the lighter textured cake. But not until
the introduction of chemical raising agents in the
nineteenth century did the recipes evolve as we know
them today, giving a whole new dimension to the art of
baking.

Tea was a drink introduced to Edinburgh in 1681 by
Mary of Modena when her husband, the future James
VII, was Duke of York and Lord High Commissioner at
the Court of Holyrood. It quickly became fashionable
but was frowned upon by both medical and clerical men

Five-piece silver tea and coffee set,
1874, Glasgow.

as bad for the body and the soul. Many ministers of the kirk considered it a greater evil than whisky, and some people resolved the quandary by adding a dram of whisky to their cup of tea to counteract its bad effects. Cinnamon was also sometimes added to enhance the flavour. So quickly did tea become popular that by the middle of the century it had replaced ale or spirits as the morning beverage, and the practice of tea drinking as a social pastime in the morning and afternoon was considered by the self-righteous to be a great time waster. Good quality tea remained expensive, however, and the customs duty high, so a lot of cheaper tea was smuggled in from the Continent, and simulated teas were manufactured from the leaves of local trees, such as hawthorn, ash or sloe. These were coloured and mixed with China tea to make a product known as smouch.

Coffee houses had long been popular meeting places for men but in 1884 an enterprising young lady named Miss Cranston opened the first of her famous tea rooms in Glasgow, and the practice of going to take tea in a public place became an enjoyable and socially acceptable one, so much so that she was able to open a number of similar establishments and the fashion soon spread throughout Britain.

Plain Scones

Makes 8

8 oz plain flour (2 cups)

a pinch of salt

1 level teaspoon bicarbonate of soda

1½ level teaspoons cream of tartar

1 oz butter (2 tablespoons)

milk

Sift the flour, salt, bicarbonate of soda and cream of tartar into a bowl. Rub in the butter and when it is evenly distributed mix in sufficient milk to make a soft but not sticky dough. Turn the dough onto a floured surface and knead it lightly, then roll the dough out to a thickness of about three-quarters of an inch and cut out as many scones as possible, using a 2½-inch cutter. Gather up the scraps and re-roll them to cut out more scones. Bake the scones at Gas 7/425°F/220°C for 10 minutes or until well risen and golden brown. Cool on a wire tray.

Fruit Scones

Mix 2½ oz (5 tablespoons) caster sugar and 2 oz (⅓ cup) dried fruit into the dry ingredients before the milk is added to make a dough. Continue as for Plain Scones.

Cheese Scones

Stir 2 oz (½ cup) grated cheese with a pinch of cayenne pepper and dry mustard into the dry ingredients, then make into a dough and continue as for Plain Scones.

Treacle Scones

Makes 8

8 oz plain flour (2 cups)

1 level teaspoon bicarbonate of soda

1 level teaspoon cream of tartar

1 level teaspoon ground ginger

½ level teaspoon mixed spice

2 oz margarine (¼ cup)

1 level tablespoon black treacle

milk

Sieve the dry ingredients into a bowl. Heat the margarine and treacle until melted and stir the liquid into the flour with enough milk to make a soft dough.

Turn it onto a floured surface and knead it lightly. Divide the dough in half and roll each piece into a circle about half an inch deep. Cut them into four farls (triangles) then either bake them at Gas 6/400°F/200°C for 12–15 minutes or cook them on a floured girdle for about 5 minutes on each side.

Serve slightly warm with butter.

Oatmeal Scones

Makes 7–8

6 oz plain flour (1½ cups)

2 oz medium oatmeal (⅓ cup)

a pinch of salt

1 level teaspoon bicarbonate of soda

2 level teaspoons cream of tartar

2 oz margarine (¼ cup)

about ¼ pint milk (⅔ cup)

Glamis Castle, Angus

Sift the flour, salt, bicarbonate of soda and cream of tartar into a bowl and stir in the oatmeal. Add the margarine cut into small pieces, rub it into the flour and when it is evenly distributed stir in sufficient milk to make a soft but not sticky dough. Turn the dough onto a floured surface and knead it lightly until smooth, then either roll the dough out and cut it into rounds using a 2½-inch fluted cutter or shape it into an 8-inch circle and cut it into eight wedges.

Bake the rounds at Gas 7/425°F/220°C for 10 minutes, or cook the wedges on a heated girdle also for about 10 minutes, but turning them halfway through the cooking time so they are golden brown on both sides. Serve oatmeal scones with butter.

Wholewheat Scones

Makes about 8

6 oz wholewheat flour (1½ cups)

2 oz plain flour (½ cup)

1 level teaspoon bicarbonate of soda

2 level teaspoons cream of tartar

a pinch of salt

2 oz butter (¼ cup)

about ¼ pint milk (⅔ cup)

Sift the plain flour, bicarbonate of soda, cream of tartar and salt into a bowl, stir in the wholewheat flour then add the butter cut into pieces. Rub the butter into the flour until evenly distributed, then stir in sufficient milk to make a soft but not sticky dough. Turn the dough onto a floured surface and knead it lightly until smooth. Roll the dough out to a thickness of about half an inch then cut out as many 2½-inch rounds as possible. Put them onto a baking tray, gather up the scraps and re-roll them to cut out more scones.

Brush the tops with milk and bake at Gas 7/425°F/220°C for about 10 minutes until golden brown and well risen.

Serve warm with butter. Wholewheat scones are especially good with cheese.

Potato Scones

This is a heavier scone, as it contains no chemical raising agent.

Makes about 8

½ lb mashed potato

½ oz butter (1 tablespoon)

2 oz plain flour (½ cup)

seasoning

While the potatoes are still warm work in the butter with plenty of seasoning, then knead in as much flour as the potato will take to make a pliable dough. Roll the dough out thinly then cut it into 3-inch rounds and prick the surface with a fork.

Heat a girdle or heavy frying pan, brush the surface with oil and cook the scones about four at a time for 3 minutes on each side or until golden brown. Keep the cooked ones warm while browning the rest.

Serve potato scones immediately with extra butter.

Drop Scones

These are sometimes known as Scotch Pancakes.

Heat a girdle or heavy based frying pan.

Sift the flour, salt, cream of tartar and bicarbonate of soda together, then stir in the caster sugar. Make a well in the centre and add the egg and a little of the milk. Gradually mix the flour into the liquid, adding more milk as you work, until the mixture is of a thick batter consistency.

Drop a spoonful of the batter onto the greased girdle to make sure it is at the correct temperature. Bubbles should rise to the surface after only a few seconds. When the underside is brown and the bubbles start to burst turn the scone over and cook the other side. Cook the scones in batches, keeping them warm in a tea towel while cooking the rest of the mixture. The girdle may require re-greasing after each batch of 3 or 4 scones.

Serve the drop scones warm with butter and honey or jam. It is also a great favourite amongst the children to butter them hot then sprinkle over brown sugar.

8 oz plain flour (2 cups)

a pinch of salt

1 level teaspoon cream of tartar

1 level teaspoon bicarbonate of soda

2 level dessertspoons caster sugar (5 teaspoons)

1 standard egg (size 3)

about ¼ pint milk (⅔ cup)

Scots Crumpets

Unlike English crumpets, these contain no yeast. They are very much thinner and can be spread with butter and jam and rolled up before serving.

Beat the egg yolks then mix in the sifted flour, salt and sugar with the melted butter and milk to make a smooth batter the consistency of thin cream. Whisk the egg whites until at the soft peak stage then lightly and quickly fold them into the batter.

Heat a girdle or frying pan and grease the surface lightly, then drop in a large tablespoonful at a time, rolling the pan so that the base is thinly coated with batter. When it is golden brown underneath turn the crumpet over to cook the other side. As the crumpets are cooked stack them in a clean tea towel. When cool spread with butter and honey or jam, then roll them up and serve immediately.

Makes about 16

8 oz plain flour (2 cups)

2 large eggs (size 2), separated

2 level tablespoons caster sugar

2 tablespoons melted butter

salt

¾ pint milk (scant 2 cups)

Selkirk Bannock

This old traditional bannock was made famous by a baker named Robbie Douglas who opened a bakery in Selkirk Market Place in the middle of the nineteenth century and produced bannocks of such excellence that they achieved worldwide renown. This bannock was a favourite with Queen Victoria who, when confronted with a rich repast during a visit to Abbotsford, asked for nothing more than a slice of Selkirk Bannock and a cup of tea.

8 oz plain strong flour (2 cups)

a pinch of salt

1 oz lard (2 tablespoons)

¼ pint milk (⅔ cup)

1 oz caster sugar (2 tablespoons)

¼ oz fresh yeast (¼ cake compressed yeast)

4 oz butter (½ cup)

2 oz cleaned currants (¼ cup)

2 oz cleaned sultanas (¼ cup)

2 oz mixed peel, chopped (¼ cup)

For the glaze

1 tablespoon water

1 level tablespoon sugar

Sieve the flour and salt into a bowl and rub in the lard. Warm the milk to blood heat then crumble in the yeast and stir until dissolved. Mix the sugar into the dry ingredients, then pour in the yeast liquid and stir the ingredients together to form a soft but not sticky dough. Turn it onto a working surface and knead it for about 5 minutes until smooth. Prove the dough in a clean greased bowl in a warm place covered with a piece of polythene for about 1 hour, until doubled in size.

When the dough is ready knock it back gently to its original size then work in the butter; currants, sultanas and mixed peel. You may need a little extra flour as the dough can become sticky. Form it into a 7-inch round, put it on a greased baking tray and leave it in a warm place for about 20 minutes to prove again. Then bake at Gas 7/425°F/220°C for 10 minutes, reduce the heat to Gas 4/350°F/180°C and bake for about 40 minutes until the bannock is well risen and golden brown.

Leave it to cool slightly. In the meantime, dissolve the sugar in the water for the glaze and boil it for a minute. Brush the glaze over the bannock and leave it to cool completely.

Serve Selkirk bannock sliced and spread with butter if liked.

Facing page: Craigievar Castle, Aberdeenshire, dating from 1626

Soda Loaf

This is also known as Buttermilk Loaf. If buttermilk or soured milk is not available stir 1 dessertspoon of white vinegar into ½ pint of milk.

1 lb plain flour (3½–4 cups)

1 level teaspoon salt

1 level teaspoon bicarbonate of soda

about ½ pint buttermilk or sour milk (1¼ cups)

Sieve the flour, salt and bicarbonate of soda into a bowl. Stir in the buttermilk or soured milk to make a soft but not sticky dough. Turn it onto a floured surface and knead it lightly.

Shape the dough into an 8-inch round and mark it into eight pieces. Alternatively the dough can be cooked in a loaf tin. Bake the bread at Gas 6/400°F/200°C for 30–40 minutes or until brown.

Fruit Loaf

14 oz plain flour (3½ cups)

2 level teaspoons baking powder

1 level teaspoon bicarbonate of soda

4 oz margarine (½ cup)

8 oz caster sugar (1 cup)

4 oz seedless raisins (⅔ cup)

4 oz currants (½ cup)

4 oz sultanas (½ cup)

1 oz mixed peel, chopped (2½ tablespoons)

½ pint sour milk (1¼ cups) or add 1 dessertspoon (2 teaspoons) vinegar to fresh milk

a 2-lb loaf tin, greased and base lined

Sift the flour, baking powder and bicarbonate of soda into a bowl. Rub in the margarine until evenly distributed then stir in the sugar together with the dried fruits. Bind the mixture together with the milk to make a soft consistency.

Turn the mixture into the tin and bake the loaf at Gas 4/350°F/180°C for 1 hour. Reduce the heat to Gas 3/325°F/160°C and bake for a further hour or until the loaf is cooked.

Keep the loaf in an airtight tin for two days before serving cut into thick slices and spread with butter.

Gingerbread

Gingerbread was a luxury sweetmeat during the middle ages because it contained expensive spices. The early version was a hard biscuit made from breadcrumbs, honey and spices, kneaded together. By the eighteenth century the crumbs had been replaced by flour, and sugar, butter, eggs, black treacle and preserved fruits were added. It was still a heavy, unleavened bread, but by the nineteenth century bicarbonate of soda was introduced as a raising agent to give us the rich, dark, moist cake we know today. There are many local recipes in Scotland. Edinburgh gingerbread includes split almonds and eggs while Fochabers has the addition of beer, sultanas, currants, peel and ground almonds. Here are just three of the many versions to be found.

Fochabers Gingerbread

8 oz plain flour (2 cups)

2 oz lard ($\frac{1}{4}$ cup)

2 oz margarine ($\frac{1}{4}$ cup)

2 oz caster sugar ($\frac{1}{4}$ cup)

2 oz mixed peel ($\frac{1}{4}$ cup)

2 oz cleaned sultanas ($\frac{1}{4}$ cup)

2 oz cleaned currants ($\frac{1}{4}$ cup)

2 oz ground almonds (scant $\frac{1}{2}$ cup)

1 level teaspoon mixed spice

2 level teaspoons ground ginger

1 level teaspoon ground cinnamon

4 oz black treacle, melted

1 large egg (size 2)

$\frac{1}{4}$ pint beer ($\frac{2}{3}$ cup)

1 level teaspoon bicarbonate of soda

a $7\frac{1}{2}$-inch cake tin, greased and base lined

Cream the margarine and lard together then add the sugar and beat the mixture until it is soft and fluffy. Add the melted treacle and gradually beat in the egg. Sift the flour together with the mixed spice, ground ginger and cinnamon and fold them into the mixture with the mixed peel, sultanas, currants and ground almonds. Dissolve the bicarbonate of soda in the beer and stir it into the other ingredients, then turn the cake mixture into the tin, spread it to the sides and hollow out the centre slightly.

Bake at Gas 2/300°F/150°C for about $1\frac{1}{2}$ hours. Cool the gingerbread in the tin for 15 minutes then turn it onto a wire tray to cool completely.

Parkin

4 oz butter (½ cup)

4 oz honey (⅓ cup)

4 oz dark soft brown sugar (½ cup, firmly packed)

1 large egg (size 2)

4 oz self-raising flour (1 cup)

4 oz medium oatmeal (⅔ cup)

1 level teaspoon ground ginger

1 level teaspoon ground cinnamon

6 tablespoons milk

a 6½-inch square tin, greased and base lined

In Scotland oatmeal was sometimes added to the gingerbread mix, and Parkin is a ginger cake made of oatmeal, spices and honey, treacle or syrup. This recipe uses honey.

Melt the butter, honey and sugar together over a low heat. Leave to cool.

Sift the flour, ginger and cinnamon into a bowl, stir in the oatmeal and add the melted mixture with the egg, well beaten, and the milk. Pour the mixture into the tin then bake at Gas 3/325°F/160°C for 1¼ hours or until the cake feels springy to the touch and is slightly shrinking away from the sides of the tin.

Turn the parkin onto a wire tray to cool then store it for one day at least before serving it sliced and buttered.

Sticky Gingerbread

6 oz plain flour (1½ cups)

1 level dessertspoon ground ginger (2 teaspoons)

1½ level teaspoons ground cinnamon

1 level teaspoon bicarbonate of soda

4 oz butter (½ cup)

4 oz soft brown sugar (½ cup, firmly packed)

4 level tablespoons black treacle

¼ pint milk (⅔ cup)

1 standard egg (size 3)

a 2-lb loaf tin, greased and base lined

Melt the butter, sugar and treacle in a pan. Sift the flour, ground ginger and cinnamon then stir the melted mixture into it with the egg, well beaten. Warm the milk to blood heat, pour it onto the bicarbonate of soda and stir it in, then add it to the main mixture.

Turn the mixture into the tin and bake at Gas 2/300°F/150°C for about 1½ hours until it is well risen. If it starts to brown too quickly cover the top with a piece of greaseproof paper.

Leave the gingerbread to cool in the tin then store it for a day before serving it sliced and spread with butter.

Seed Cake

8 oz butter (1 cup)

6 oz caster sugar (¾ cup)

3 standard eggs (size 3)

8 oz self-raising flour (2 cups)

½ level teaspoon ground nutmeg

½ oz caraway seeds

2 tablespoons fresh orange juice

a 7-inch square tin greased and base lined

Caraway seed is sometimes called carvi in Scotland, as it is in France.

Cream the butter and sugar together until light and fluffy in colour and texture. Add the eggs gradually, beating well between each addition, then stir in the caraway seeds with the orange juice.

Sift the flour and nutmeg together then fold it into the creamed mixture. Turn the cake mixture into the tin, spread it to the sides and hollow out the centre.

Bake the cake at Gas 5/375°F/190°C for about 45 minutes or until golden brown and springy to the touch.

Cool the cake on a wire tray.

Diet Cake

8 oz caster sugar (1 cup)

4 large eggs (size 2)

½ level teaspoon ground cinnamon

the grated rind of half a lemon

6 oz plain flour (1½ cups)

an 8-inch round cake tin

The recipe was mentioned by Scott in *St Ronan's Well*. It is based on Scots Diet Loaf published in *The Cook and Housewife's Manual* by Mrs Margaret Dods in 1826.

Line the base and sides of the tin with greaseproof paper and grease the lining.

Using a mixer or with the bowl suspended over a pan of hot water whisk the eggs and sugar together until they are light and creamy and a definite trail is left in the mixture when the whisk is removed from the bowl. Sift the flour and lightly and carefully fold it into the mixture with the ground cinnamon and lemon rind.

Turn the mixture into the prepared tin, sprinkle a little extra caster sugar over the surface and bake the cake at Gas 6/400°F/200°C for about 40 minutes until well risen and golden brown.

The sugar sprinkled over the surface may be omitted and the cake iced when cold.

Dundee Cake

This is the most important cake of the Scottish tea table and is served at celebrations such as christenings and birthdays. It is distinguishable from other fruit cakes by its almond-strewn top.

4 oz cleaned sultanas (½ cup)

4 oz cleaned currants (½ cup)

4 oz cleaned and stoned raisins (½ cup)

2 oz mixed peel, chopped (¼ cup)

3 oz glacé cherries, chopped (6 tablespoons)

2 oz ground almonds (scant ½ cup)

9 oz plain flour (2¼ cups)

8 oz butter (1 cup)

1 level teaspoon baking powder

8 oz caster sugar (1 cup)

3 standard eggs (size 3)

1 tablespoon sherry or milk

1 oz almonds blanched and halved (3 tablespoons)

grated rind of 1 lemon

a 7-inch cake tin

Grease and line the base and sides of the tin and grease the paper lining.

Mix the sultanas, currants, raisins, peel, cherries and ground almonds together.

Beat the butter until it is soft and creamy then add the caster sugar and beat the mixture with the lemon rind until light and fluffy in both colour and texture. Beat the eggs together then add them gradually to the creamed mixture, beating well between each addition. Sift together the flour and baking powder and lightly stir it into the creamed mixture with the milk or sherry and all the dried fruit.

Turn the mixture into the tin, spread it to the sides and slightly hollow out the centre, then cover the surface with the almonds.

Bake the cake at Gas 3/325°F/160°C for 2½–3 hours or until a warm skewer pushed into the mixture comes out clean.

Cool the cake in the tin for 15 minutes then turn it out onto a wire tray to cool completely.

Marmalade Cake

6 oz margarine (¾ cup)

3 oz caster sugar (⅓ cup)

2 large eggs (size 2)

6 level tablespoons thick cut marmalade

8 oz self-raising flour (2 cups)

4 oz cleaned sultanas (½ cup)

a 7-inch cake tin greased and base lined

Cream the margarine until soft, then add the sugar and beat the two ingredients together until light and fluffy in both colour and texture. Add the eggs one at a time, beating well between each addition. Mix in the marmalade and sultanas and lastly stir in the sifted flour.

Turn the mixture into the tin, level the surface and bake the cake at Gas 4/350°F/180°C for 1–1½ hours or until a warmed skewer inserted into the cake comes out clean. If any mixture adheres to the skewer cook the cake for a little longer.

Cool the cake in the tin for 15 minutes then turn it onto a wire tray to cool completely.

Honey Buns

Makes 14

3 oz honey (¼ cup)

2 oz granulated sugar (¼ cup)

2 oz margarine (4 tablespoons)

4 oz plain flour (1 cup)

1 oz chopped walnuts (3 tablespoons)

1 oz ground almonds (scant 4 tablespoons)

½ level teaspoon bicarbonate of soda

1 standard egg (size 3)

For the icing

4 oz sifted icing sugar (1 cup)

1 oz walnuts, finely chopped (3 tablespoons)

patty tins, lightly greased

Honey was used as a sweetener long before sugar was imported from the West Indies, and bee-keeping was practised from the earliest Celtic times. Scottish heather honey has an unsurpassed reputation. Do try these light, melt-in-the-mouth honey buns.

Put the honey, granulated sugar and margarine into a pan and over a low heat melt them together – the mixture must not boil. Sift together the flour and bicarbonate of soda and stir them into the melted mixture with the chopped walnuts, ground almonds and egg. When the ingredients are well combined, divide the mixture between the patty tins, filling each just over half full.

Bake the buns at Gas 4/350°F/180°C for about 15 minutes or until well risen and golden brown.

Transfer them to a wire tray to cool before icing.

Mix the icing sugar with enough warm water to make a stiff consistency. Ice the top of each bun and decorate with a few chopped walnuts before serving for tea.

Abernethy Biscuits

Makes 20
8 oz plain flour (2 cups)
½ level teaspoon baking powder
3 oz butter (6 tablespoons)
3 oz caster sugar (⅓ cup)
½ level teaspoon caraway seeds
1 tablespoon milk
1 standard egg (size 3)

These biscuits are said to have taken their name not from the Perthshire burgh but from a Dr John Abernethy. Apparently he regularly lunched at a baker's where he ate ordinary plain biscuits, but after his suggestion of adding caraway seeds and sugar was adopted, the new biscuits were named after him.

Sift the flour and baking powder into a bowl, add the butter and rub it in until evenly distributed. Stir in the sugar and caraway seeds then bind the mixture together with the egg and milk to make a fairly stiff dough.

Turn the dough onto a floured surface and roll it out thinly. Then cut out the biscuits with a 3-inch plain cutter and gather up the trimmings to make more rounds. Place the biscuits on greased baking trays and bake at Gas 5/375°F/190°C for about 10 minutes until light golden brown. Cool, then serve for tea.

Crathes Castle, Kincardineshire: the Tower Room

Gingerbread Men

In Scotland these biscuits, favourites with the children, are sometimes called Gingerbread Husbands.

Sieve the flour, a pinch of salt and the ginger into a bowl. Melt the margarine, sugar and syrup together then stir them into the dry ingredients to form a pliable dough. Leave it on one side until firm and cool enough to handle.

On a lightly floured work surface roll the dough out to a thickness of about a quarter of an inch and cut as many gingerbread men as possible using the cutter. Gather up the scraps and re-roll them for more biscuits.

Place the men on greased baking trays and decorate each with currants for buttons and a small piece of cherry for the mouth. Bake the biscuits at Gas 4/350°F/180°C for 15 minutes or until golden brown. Leave to cool slightly then transfer to a wire tray to cool completely.

Makes about 15

10 oz self raising flour (2½ cups)

2 oz margarine (¼ cup)

4 oz caster sugar (½ cup)

3 level teaspoons ground ginger

3 heaped tablespoons golden syrup

glacé cherries and currants for decoration

a gingerbread man cutter

Melting Moments

Cream the margarine and lard together, add the caster sugar and continue beating until the mixture is light and fluffy. Beat in the egg then gradually stir in the flour with the vanilla essence to make a stiff dough.

Using slightly wet hands roll the mixture into small balls about the size of shelled walnuts. Roll each ball in the oats then place them on baking trays, not too closely together as they spread slightly during cooking. Flatten each biscuit a little then bake at Gas 5/375°F/190°C for about 15 minutes until golden brown.

Cool on a wire tray.

Makes 24–28

5 oz margarine (10 tablespoons)

3 oz lard (6 tablespoons)

6 oz caster sugar (¾ cup)

10 oz self-raising flour (2½ cups)

1 large egg (size 2)

2 teaspoons vanilla essence

about 4 oz rolled oats (1 cup)

Petticoat Tails

There are various theories as to the origin of these curiously-named shortbread biscuits. Some say the name was derived from the French *Petites Gatelles*, meaning little cakes; others that its origin lies in the shape of the biscuits which is a replica of the Elizabethan full gored skirt; while a third possibility is that it was the clever invention of a cook after years of broken tips to triangular-shaped biscuits.

12 oz plain flour (3 cups)

6 oz butter (¾ cup)

2 oz caster sugar (¼ cup)

4 tablespoons milk

Sift the flour into a bowl and stir in the sugar. Gently heat the butter and milk together and as soon as the butter has melted stir the liquid into the flour to make a soft but not sticky dough.

Turn it onto a floured surface and knead it lightly. Divide the dough in half then roll the halves out directly onto a baking tray into 9-inch rounds using a large plate as a guide. Flute the edges.

Cut out a 2-inch circle from the centre but leave it in place. Divide the outer ring into eight, keeping the inner circle whole. Sprinkle with caster sugar and bake at Gas 4/350°F/180°C for about 30 minutes or until golden brown and crisp.

Pitcaithly Bannock

6 oz plain flour (1½ cups)

1 oz cornflour (¼ cup)

1½ oz citron peel, chopped (you can buy this preserved lemon peel in a piece)

3 oz caster sugar (⅓ cup)

1 oz almonds, blanched and chopped (3 tablespoons)

4 oz butter (½ cup)

Sift the flours into a bowl. Add the almonds and peel.

Cream the butter and sugar together until soft then add the sifted flours with the almonds and peel and knead the ingredients together to form a dough.

Roll it out to an 8-inch round, pinch the edges and mark the dough into eight wedges (farls). Transfer to a baking tray. Bake at Gas 2/300°F/150°C for 45–50 minutes. Cool on a wire tray then sprinkle with caster sugar.

Highlanders

This recipe comes from Cringletie House Hotel at Eddleston, near Peebles. The hotel is a distinctive mansion built of red sandstone in Scottish baronial style. Mr and Mrs Stanley Maguire are joint proprietors and Mrs Maguire is in charge of the kitchen.

Makes 20

2 oz caster sugar ($\frac{1}{4}$ cup)

4 oz butter ($\frac{1}{2}$ cup)

5 oz plain flour ($1\frac{1}{4}$ cups)

2 oz Farola ($\frac{1}{2}$ cup)

milk

demerara sugar

Preheat the oven to Gas 8/450°F/230°C. Grease a baking sheet.

Cream the caster sugar and butter until light and fluffy. Lightly mix in the flour and Farola. Roll the mixture into a long sausage shape. Brush well with milk and roll in demerara sugar. Slice into 20 pieces. Arrange these on the baking sheet and place in the centre of the oven. Bake for about 20 minutes.

Shortbread

Shortbread is now eaten throughout the year, although traditionally it was associated with the Christmas and Hogmanay time. The large round biscuit is derived from the ancient Yule Bannock, which was notched around the edge to signify the sun's rays.

There are many different local versions of the basic mixture: in Edinburgh it is decorated with slivers of peel and almonds, while in Ayrshire it is enriched with cream and eggs. In the Shetland and Orkney Islands it contains caraway seeds and is known as Bride's Bonn.

Makes 2

7 oz plain flour ($1\frac{3}{4}$ cups)

1 oz rice flour ($\frac{1}{4}$ cup)

4 oz butter ($\frac{1}{2}$ cup)

2 oz caster sugar ($\frac{1}{4}$ cup)

Mix the flour, rice flour and sugar together. Add the butter cut into pieces and using the finger tips rub it in until evenly distributed, then knead the mixture together to form a soft but not sticky dough.

Divide the dough in half and using either an oiled and sugared shortbread mould or just your hands shape it into two rounds. They should be about three-quarters of an inch thick. Decorate the edges if not using the mould, then place the rounds on greased baking trays and bake at Gas 3/325°F/160°C for about 45 minutes or until brown. Cool.

*Shortbread stamped from a thistle
mould*

Blackcurrant Jam

Makes about 8 lb
3 lb blackcurrants (12 cups)
2¼ pints cold water (5½ cups)
4½ lb granulated sugar (10 cups)
1 oz butter (2 tablespoons)

Strip the blackcurrants from their stem, then wash the fruit
and put it into a preserving pan. Add the water and simmer
covered for 15 to 20 minutes or until tender. Stir in the sugar
and when every grain has dissolved bring the jam to a
rolling boil and boil it rapidly until setting point is reached
(see Apricot Jam, page 101).

Stir in the butter when the jam is ready, then leave it for
about 10 minutes so the fruit is evenly dispersed. Pour into
clean warm jars, cover, label and store.

Apricot Jam

Makes 5½ lb

1 lb dried apricots, washed and roughly chopped (3 cups)

2 lemons

2 pints water (5 cups)

1 oz almonds, blanched and chopped (¼ cup)

3½ lb granulated sugar (8 cups)

Put the apricots into a bowl and add the lemon rind and juice. Tie the lemon pips in a piece of muslin and put them in with the water. Leave to soak for 24 hours.

Rub a little butter around the inside of the preserving pan. Put in it the soaked apricots, the bag of pips and the liquid and over a low heat bring it to the boil. Cover the pan and simmer the fruit for about 15 minutes or until tender.

Remove the bag of pips, add the sugar and when every grain has melted boil the jam rapidly for 20–25 minutes, stirring it occasionally to avoid sticking. Test the jam for set by placing a spoonful on a plate, letting it cool and then pushing the surface with your finger. If it wrinkles the jam is ready.

Stir in the almonds then cool the preserve for 10 minutes to prevent the fruit rising.

Ladle into clean warm jars, cover, label and store until required.

Strawberry Jam

Makes 7 lb

4 lb strawberries

the juice of 1 large lemon

1 oz butter (2 tablespoons)

4 lb preserving sugar (9 cups)

Select fresh and slightly under-ripe fruit, remove the stalks and put the strawberries into a large pan with the lemon juice. Cover the fruit and simmer it gently for about 15 minutes until the fruit is soft. Press the fruit against the sides of the pan to extract all the juice. Stir in the sugar and when it has dissolved bring the jam to a rolling boil and boil it steadily for about 10 minutes. Test for set as in Apricot Jam (this page).

Stir in the butter, then leave the jam to stand for 10 minutes so the fruit settles. Pour into warm, clean jars, cover, label and store.

Blaeberry Jam

Blaeberries are also known as bilberries or whortleberries.

Makes 3 lb
2 lb blaeberries
½ lb rhubarb
2 lb preserving sugar (4 cups)

Wash, trim and roughly chop the rhubarb. Put it into a pan and cook gently until it starts to soften. Stir in the sugar and when it has dissolved add the blaeberries and bring the jam to the boil. Boil it rapidly for up to 20 minutes to setting point (see Apricot Jam, page 101). Cool slightly then pour into clean warm jars, cover, label and store.

Gooseberry Jam

Makes about 5 lb
3 lb slightly under-ripe gooseberries (12 cups)
1 pint cold water (2¼ cups)
3 lb granulated sugar (6 cups)

Top and tail the gooseberries with a pair of scissors, then put the fruit into a pan with the water. Bring the liquid to the boil, slowly using a wooden spoon to crush the fruit against the side of the pan to help extract as much of the juice as possible. Cook the fruit gently until tender, about 20 minutes.

Stir in the sugar and when every grain has melted bring the jam to a rapid boil and continue to boil it for about 10 minutes or until setting point is reached (see Apricot Jam, page 101). Pour the jam into clean warm jars after it has cooled for about 10 minutes, then seal, label and store.

Makes 7 lb
4 lb raspberries
4 lb sugar (9 cups)

Raspberry Jam

Remove the stalks, if any, from the fruit, put the raspberries into a pan and over a low heat soften the fruit for 15–20 minutes. Stir in the sugar and when every grain has melted bring the jam to the boil and boil it rapidly for about 10 minutes. Test for set (see Apricot Jam, page 101) then leave the preserve for about 15 minutes to cool slightly and for the fruit to settle. Pour the jam into clean, warm jars. Cover, label and store until required.

Sloe and Apple Jelly

Makes 4 lb
2 lb sloes (or damsons)
2 lb cooking apples
2 lb sugar (4 cups)

The superb Adam dining room at Culzean Castle, Ayrshire

Wash the sloes and prick them if they are picked before the first frost. Put them into a pan. Wash and roughly chop the apples and add them to the sloes, then pour in enough cold water to cover.

Bring the liquid to the boil, reduce the heat and simmer for about 40 minutes or until both fruits are really soft.

Scald the jelly bag, suspend it over a bowl and pour in the fruit and liquid. Leave the liquid to drip through overnight, but do not be tempted to squeeze the bag as this will make the jelly cloudy.

Next day measure the liquid and add 1 lb sugar for every pint (2 cups per 2½ cups liquid). Warm the liquid, stir in the sugar and melt it over a low heat, then bring the jelly to the boil and boil it rapidly for about 10 minutes or until setting point is reached. Test for set as in Apricot Jam, page 101. Pour the jelly into warm clean jars, cover, label and store.

Lemon Curd

Makes about 2½ lb

4 large eggs (size 2), beaten

the juice and finely grated rind of 4 large lemons

8 oz butter (1 cup)

12 oz caster sugar (1½ cups)

Cut the butter into small pieces and put it into a double saucepan or a bowl suspended over a pan of simmering water. Add the sugar, lemon rind and juice and stir the mixture over the heat until it has melted together.

Stirring constantly, pour a little of the mixture into the beaten eggs then return all the ingredients to the pan or bowl and stir them until the preserve thickens. It should lightly coat the back of a wooden spoon. It may take up to 10 minutes to reach the correct consistency.

Put the lemon curd in warm clean jars, cover, label and store in a cool place until required.

Facing page: Cold dressed salmon

Overleaf: Forth Lobster Lady Tweedsmuir

Food for Kings

The most luxurious of Scotland's native foods have not always been treated with the reverence in which they are held today, but now her abundant riches have been exploited and exported and bring important revenue to the country. Game was not in fact shot for sport until the nineteenth century, and the much-prized grouse and pheasant were only used to augment the stock-pot in the absence of anything better. Nowadays many of Scotland's large estates are owned or the shooting rights rented by a syndicate, and the young birds are carefully reared and released to be shot for sport. Hunting used to be the favourite sport of kings, and great formal deer hunts were organised by the Highland chiefs. Mary Queen of Scots was royally entertained by the Earl of Atholl at a number of these hunting parties. Again by the nineteenth century the hunting of deer was replaced by stalking, which is a private affair between huntsman, stalker and beast. So valuable are game birds, beasts and fish that laws have had to be passed limiting the catching of them to certain times of the year, so that stocks can be replenished during the closed, breeding seasons. People will pay vast sums of money for the

Grouse shooting: an engraving of 1798

privilege of attending a grouse shoot or fishing a salmon river, coming from the Continent and the United States to do so. The produce commands high prices, particularly at the beginning of the season when the young creatures are at their most succulent and tender.

Yet only a century ago so common a fish was the salmon that servants who lived in had a clause in their contracts stipulating that salmon would not be served to them more than three times a week, and at one time in the late eighteenth century the River Girvan was so overstocked with salmon that the fish were used to manure the fields! Now each river has its own seasonal dates, but these generally cover early February to late August, and the fish caught during the first fortnight of this season are considered to be the finest.

It is frequently forgotten that the famous roast beef of old England is very often from Scotland, for Scotch beef has a reputation for being the finest in the British Isles. The principle species are the Aberdeen Angus, thought to have been introduced to Scotland by the Vikings, and the Galloway, which is a lowland cattle. In Georgian times it became the practice to rear Galloway

Deer stalking: an engraving of 1840

Grouse shoot near Braemar

in Scotland and then drive them south to the country round London for fattening and slaughtering. In Scotland mutton is eaten more than in England, where young lamb is preferred, but the mountain mutton which has been grazing on the aromatic native herbs has an unsurpassable flavour.

With such a wealth of fine produce culinary embellishment is not necessary, but the French chefs who were imported to Scotland during the period of the Auld Alliance devised many elaborate recipes. No upper class house in Edinburgh was without a French chef if it could afford one, although for some time these new

'Salmon and Brown Trout', H. L.
Rolfe (1847–1881)

culinary fashions remained confined to the circles surrounding the court at Holyrood. No expense was spared in the preparation of a lavish table, and as the chefs felt that a sputtering fire imparted a special flavour to their creations, several pounds of butter might be used daily in one house by kitchen hands who fed the flames with mops dipped in melted butter. Eggs and cream were much favoured in this type of cooking, and the desserts which came into fashion during the sixteenth and seventeenth centuries were based on these ingredients and bore such delightful names as Whim Wham, Edinburgh Fog, Scotch Mist and Floating Islands. An egg and cream liaison was also used for thickening the more refined soups and sauces at the aristocratic table, in contrast to the oatmeal thickening of the humbler broths and broses.

By the eighteenth century adventurous cooking had become the craze for its own sake, and chefs vied with one another to produce exotic concoctions made of cows' palates or udders, of ox eyes and cocks' combs! Fortunately the more preposterous of these conceits have been abandoned, and we are left with a bill of fare in which the very finest of foodstuffs have been explored by the most skilful of culinary artists. The result is sheer gastronomic delight.

Game Soup

Serves 6

For the game stock

game bones or an old grouse or pheasant

2 oz butter ($\frac{1}{4}$ cup)

2 rashers streaky bacon, roughly chopped

1 large carrot, peeled and roughly chopped

1 large onion, peeled and roughly chopped

1 bay leaf

6 peppercorns

4 pints water (10 cups)

To complete the soup

8 oz turnip, peeled and evenly diced

8 oz carrot, peeled and evenly diced

2 oz butter ($\frac{1}{4}$ cup)

1 oz plain flour ($\frac{1}{4}$ cup)

3 pints game stock ($7\frac{1}{2}$ cups)

2 tablespoons sherry

This is an ideal soup to make if you have an old grouse or pheasant or some game carcasses. I usually make it when I cook a game pie and have the bones from the grouse and hare, and the bones and skin of the pork can be added to the basic stock to give the soup a good flavour.

It is quite adaptable to the ingredients available, and every Highland housewife will have her own version.

Break the bones up roughly or joint the bird. Melt the butter, add the game and bacon with the chopped carrot and onion and sauté them all together until the fat is absorbed and the ingredients start to brown. Stir in the bay leaf and peppercorns, pour in the water and bring it to the boil, then cover the pan, reduce the heat and simmer the stock for about 3 hours.

When it is ready strain it and leave to cool, then pick all the meat off the bones and pound it to a smooth paste.

Melt the butter and sauté the diced carrot and turnip until starting to soften, stir in the flour and brown it lightly then gradually pour in the stock. Bring the soup to the boil, add the game and simmer the liquid for about 15 minutes.

Stir in the sherry and check for seasoning before serving.

Lorraine Soup

Serves 4–6

$\frac{1}{2}$ lb minced cooked white meat (chicken and/or veal)

2 oz blanched almonds (6 tablespoons)

2 cooked egg yolks, sieved

2 pints stock (5 cups)

1 tablespoon fresh white breadcrumbs

a pinch of nutmeg

the pared rind of half a lemon

$\frac{1}{4}$ pint single cream ($\frac{2}{3}$ cup)

Lorraine Soup is said to be named after Mary of Guise-Lorraine, the wife of James V and mother of Mary Stuart, who set the fashion for French cooking.

Put the minced meat and almonds into the liquidizer with some of the stock and blend to a smooth paste.

Turn into a pan with the rest of the stock, the sieved egg yolks, breadcrumbs, nutmeg and lemon rind. Bring the soup to the boil, then just before serving stir in the cream. Remove the piece of lemon peel and check the soup for seasoning before serving.

Feather Fowlie

The name derives from the French *vollaille*, or chicken.

Serves 6–8

a 2½ lb roasting chicken, jointed
1 stick of celery, sliced
1 carrot, peeled and sliced
1 onion
2 oz ham, chopped (⅓ cup)
parsley stalks
1 sprig of thyme
1 blade of mace
3 pints water (7½ cups)
3 egg yolks
1 tablespoon single cream
1 level tablespoon chopped parsley

Soak the chicken joints in cold salted water for half an hour, then drain and rinse them thoroughly. Place them in a large pan, add the ham, onion, celery, carrot, parsley stalks, thyme and mace and pour in the water. Bring the soup to the boil then skim the surface, cover the pan and simmer the mixture for 1 hour. Strain the soup into a large bowl. Remove all the white chicken meat and mince it.

Remove the grease from the surface of the liquid then pour it back into a clean pan and bring it slowly to the boil. Simmer for 15 minutes then stir in the minced meat.

Beat the egg yolks and cream together, stir in a little of the hot liquid and pour the mixture into the soup. Stir it over the heat for a few minutes but do not allow it to boil. Mix in the parsley and check the soup for seasoning before pouring it into a heated tureen for serving.

Partan Bree

Serves 4–6

1 boiled crab
2 oz long grain rice
(4 tablespoons)
1 pint milk (2½ cups)
½–1 pint chicken stock
(1¼–2½ cups)
salt and pepper
a few drops anchovy essence
¼ pint single cream (⅔ cup)

Remove all the meat from the crab (see Dressed Crab, page 117) and keep on one side the pieces taken from the large claws.

Cook the rice in the milk until soft then stir in the main part of the crab meat and purée it in either a liquidizer or Mouli vegetable mill. Return the soup to a clean pan and gradually add sufficient stock to make a good consistency. Stir the soup until it boils, add the seasoning with the anchovy essence and meat from the large claws, and simmer the soup until the meat is thoroughly heated. Gradually stir in the cream but on no account let the soup boil.

Serve immediately with Melba toast.

Above: Some of the famous silver from Brodick Castle, Isle of Arran Facing page: The Great Hall of Craigievar Castle

Avocado and Cream Cheese with Fresh Herbs

Serves 8

4 avocado pears

fresh herbs to decorate

For the filling

8 oz Philadelphia cheese

2 teaspoons finely chopped parsley

2 teaspoons finely chopped lovage

2 teaspoons finely chopped sage

2 teaspoons finely chopped savoury

1 tablespoon single cream ($\frac{1}{2}$ fl oz)

salt

Here is another recipe from Cringletie House Hotel. Mrs Maguire uses a wide variety of herbs in her recipes, and here is her delicious way of serving avocado pears.

Blend together all the filling ingredients and lightly season to taste with salt.

Halve the avocado pears, remove the stones and fill with the cream cheese mixture. Decorate each with a small sprig of fresh herbs.

Auld Alliance

This deceptively simple cheese cream from Overscaig in Sutherland is delicious served as a cream pâté for the first course or at the end of a meal as a savoury.

Serves 4
¾ lb Roquefort cheese
whisky

Pound the cheese to a thick cream. Add drop by drop as much whisky as it will 'drink' to make a firm cream. Pack into small earthenware pots and chill in the fridge for 3 to 4 hours. Serve with hot buttered toast or oatcakes.

Game Pâté

Supplies of fresh meat and poultry in towns were for centuries augmented by the keeping of pigeons. The larger houses had quite sizeable dovecots, and even small cottages had a little wooden pigeon-house attached to the roof.

Serves 6–8
1 pigeon
8 oz belly of pork
4 oz streaky bacon rashers
4 oz pig's liver
6 juniper berries, crushed
6 peppercorns, crushed
1 onion, peeled and finely chopped
1 tablespoon red wine or brandy
2 oz butter (¼ cup)
1 large clove garlic, crushed
1 level tablespoon fresh chopped herbs or 1 level teaspoon dried herbs
1 standard egg (size 3) beaten
about ¼ pint aspic jelly (⅔ cup)

Remove all the meat from the pigeon, cut the skin and any bones from the pork and remove the rind and any small bones from the bacon rashers.

Chop half the pigeon and a quarter of the pork into small pieces and put them into a bowl. Mince the rest of the pigeon and pork with the pigeon liver, pig's liver and the bacon rashers, using the fine disc, and mix them into the pieces of meat.

Melt the butter and sauté the onion and garlic until soft. Stir them into the meat mixture with the herbs, egg, red wine or brandy, juniper berries and peppercorns. Add some seasoning then pack the mixture into a 1½–2 pint terrine dish. Cover it with a lid or a sheet of foil and stand the dish in a roasting tin with hot water coming half way up the sides.

Cook the pâté at Gas 2/300°F/150°C for 2 hours. Leave to cool then cover the surface with a piece of greaseproof paper and weight overnight to give a firm texture.

Heat the aspic jelly, pour it over the pâté so the surface is covered and decorate with an extra bay leaf and juniper berries.

Dressed Crab

Serves 3

1 cooked crab weighing about
3 lb (about 1½ lb crab meat)

1½ tablespoons single cream

3 level tablespoons fresh white
breadcrumbs

sieved hard boiled egg yolks

chopped parsley

salt, pepper and mustard

Twist off the large and small claws then insert your fingers into the sockets left by the large claws and pull out the centre of the crab. Remove and discard all the feathery gills, the small sac which lies at the top of the shell near the eyes and any green matter from inside the shell. Next pull off and discard the tail, then split the white hard piece and using a skewer pick out the white meat in the pockets.

Into separate bowls put the brown meat from the main shell and the white meat from the centre. With a little pressure break the edge away from the main shell following the natural line. Scrub and dry the shell well. Crack the large claws and shred the meat then mix it with the other white meat. Cream the brown meat with the cream, breadcrumbs and seasoning. Pack the white meat on either side of the shell with the brown meat down the centre.

Decorate the crab with sieved hard boiled egg yolks and chopped parsley. Arrange it on a serving plate with lettuce, radish, cucumber etc. and serve with mayonnaise or tartare sauce and brown bread and butter.

Crab Crêpes

Serves 4 (6 as a first course)
12 small thin pancakes

For the filling

8 oz crab meat, mixed

3 oz butter (6 tablespoons)

3 standard eggs (size 3)

3 tablespoons double cream

1 tablespoon Drambuie

1 tablespoon Parmesan cheese

For the sauce and topping

1 oz butter (2 tablespoons)

1 oz plain flour (¼ cup)

½ pint milk (1¼ cups)

salt and pepper

1 level tablespoon dried
breadcrumbs

½ level tablespoon Parmesan cheese

Heat the crab meat and butter together. Beat the eggs and stir them into the pan with the cream, Drambuie and cheese. Cook all these ingredients until the mixture thickens. Season.

Spread the mixture evenly between the pancakes, fold them into four and arrange them overlapping in a shallow ovenproof dish. Melt the butter for the sauce, stir in the flour then gradually blend in the milk. When the sauce is smooth, bring it to the boil, stirring constantly, and cook it until it thickens. Check for seasoning. Pour the sauce over the pancakes then sprinkle the dried breadcrumbs and cheese over the surface.

Heat the dish at Gas 4/350°F/180°C for about 20 minutes then place it quickly under a grill to brown if necessary.

Serve garnished with watercress.

Crab and Fennel Quiche

Serves 4

For the pastry

6 oz plain flour (1½ cups)

¼ teaspoon salt

1½ oz lard (3 tablespoons)

1½ oz butter (3 tablespoons)

For the filling

6 oz cooked crab meat, flaked

1 tablespoon fennel leaves, chopped

¼ pint milk (⅔ cup)

¼ pint cream (⅔ cup)

2 large eggs (size 2)

anchovy essence

salt and pepper

1 teaspoon tomato purée

This superb quiche comes from Cringletie House Hotel.

Heat the oven to Gas 6/400°F/200°C. Make the pastry in the usual way, roll out thinly and use to line a greased 7-inch flan ring.

Spread the flaked crab meat over the base of the pastry case and sprinkle with chopped fennel leaves. Lightly whisk together the milk, cream, eggs, a few drops of anchovy essence, salt, pepper and tomato purée. Pour this mixture over the crab and fennel. Bake in the centre of the oven for 15 minutes. Reduce the heat to Gas 4/350°F/180°C for a further 25 minutes, or until the quiche is golden and set.

Remove the flan ring and decorate with sprigs of fennel.

Forth Lobster Lady Tweedsmuir

Serves 4–6

2 lb cooked lobster

3 oz butter (6 tablespoons)

1 oz plain flour (¼ cup)

½ pint milk (1¼ cups)

¼ pint cream (⅔ cup)

2 standard egg yolks (size 3)

1 level tablespoon chopped parsley

1 glass Drambuie (¼ cup)

For the decoration

12 button mushrooms, wiped

2 oz butter (¼ cup)

lemon wedges

half a cucumber, sliced

This recipe is from the late Mrs Gena Mackinnon, mother of the current chairman of The Drambuie Liqueur Company.

Cut the lobster meat into pieces and leave the lobster shells in a warm place while preparing the filling.

Melt 1 oz (2 tablespoons) of the butter, stir in the flour then gradually blend in the milk. Over a medium heat, stirring constantly, bring the sauce to the boil. Mix the egg yolks and cream together, pour in a little of the hot sauce, then when it is well blended pour this back into the rest of the sauce and, stirring all the time, heat it through – do not allow the sauce to boil or it may curdle.

Melt the remaining 2 oz (¼ cup) butter in a pan, add the lobster and toss it in the hot fat, then stir in the Drambuie with the sauce and chopped parsley. Check the mixture for seasoning then turn it into the lobster shells.

Sauté the mushrooms in the butter, then arrange them around the dish with slices of cucumber and lemon wedges.

Fresh Salmon

Salmon, the king of all fish, can unfortunately be easily over-cooked, resulting in a dry, tasteless, filling fish that is sometimes very hard to digest. All cooks have their own pet theories as to the best way of cooking this magnificent fish. Here is mine. It originated from a Scottish friend and I must say I have had success every time. The method of cooking is exactly the same regardless of the size of the fish. The only determining factor is whether you have a large enough pan to fit the fish or are the fortunate owner of a fish kettle. Otherwise it can be baked in foil in the oven, following the method for salmon trout on page 120. The following method is exactly the same whether the fish is to be served hot or cold.

To poach

Wipe the fish, put it into a large pan or on the strainer of a fish kettle and fill the container with enough fresh cold water to cover. Add plenty of salt with 2 tablespoons of cider vinegar, a sprig of parsley and 6 peppercorns. Cover the pan and very slowly bring the liquid to the boil. Boil it rapidly for 3 minutes, then remove the pan from the heat.

To serve hot

With the pan well covered leave the fish in the water for 20 minutes then drain it well.

Remove the skin and serve the fish with hollandaise sauce, new potatoes and a cucumber salad.

To serve cold

Remove the lid from the pan when it has boiled for the 3 minutes and leave the fish to cool completely in the liquid.

Drain it well, remove the skin, then serve the fish, preferably on the day of cooking, garnished with lettuce, lemon twists, strips of pepper, hard boiled eggs, mustard and cress and parsley. Complete the meal with mayonnaise and buttered new potatoes if liked.

Salmon Trout

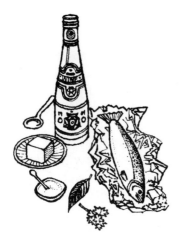

These fish weigh around 2½ lb and are best cooked whole. As so few people own fish kettles the following method of cooking the fish in the oven is very suitable, and very delicious.

Thickly butter a large piece of foil, place the salmon in the centre and fold up the edges. Add 2 tablespoons of white wine, a sprig of parsley, some salt and a bay leaf. Seal the fish well so that none of the juices can escape, then place the fish in a roasting tin and cook it at Gas 2/300°F/150°C for 45 minutes to 1 hour, depending on its size. Remove the dish from the oven and leave the fish in the foil for 10 minutes if it is to be served hot or until it is completely cool if it is to be eaten cold.

Serve as for Poached Salmon.

Salmon Steak Toravaig

Serves 4
4 salmon steaks
seasoned flour
oatmeal
1 egg, beaten
salt and pepper
1 oz butter, melted (2 tablespoons)
parsley butter (see recipe)
1 lemon, sliced

This Scottish way of grilling salmon steaks comes from Toravaig House Hotel. Salmon can be a dry fish when cooked in small pieces, and this is a particularly tasty method of retaining its natural succulence.

Wipe the salmon and remove the skin. Pass through seasoned flour, dip in beaten egg and coat with oatmeal. Brush both sides with melted butter and season. Grill both sides slowly, basting well. Garnish with parsley butter and lemon slices.

To make parsley butter simply cream 3 oz butter (6 tablespoons) until soft, then mix in 2 tablespoons chopped parsley, 1 teaspoon lemon juice and a seasoning of black pepper. Shape into a roll and chill.

Facing page: fishing on the River Tay, Dunkeld

Poacher's Salmon

Serves 4

4 salmon cutlets

¼ pint (⅔ cup) single cream

2 tablespoons Drambuie

½ teaspoon anchovy essence

salt and pepper

Place the salmon cutlets in a well-buttered ovenproof dish and sprinkle with salt and pepper. Mix the cream with the Drambuie and anchovy essence and pour it over the fish. Cover the dish loosely with foil and cook the salmon at Gas 4/350°F/180°C for 40–45 minutes or until the fish is just cooked.

Serve with buttered new potatoes and a cucumber salad.

Salmon Soufflé

Serves 4

1½ oz butter (3 tablespoons)

1½ oz plain flour (6 tablespoons)

¾ pint milk (2 cups)

1 lb cooked salmon or 2 7¾-oz cans

3 standard eggs (size 3), separated

½ oz powdered gelatine
(2 US envelopes)

3 tablespoons lemon juice

1 tablespoon Drambuie

salt and pepper

a few drops Tabasco sauce

a pinch of ground mace

¼ pint single cream (⅔ cup)

Encircle a 1½-pint soufflé dish with a sheet of foil that stands 2 inches above the rim, and fasten with tape. Melt the butter, add the flour, then gradually stir in the milk to make a smooth sauce. Over the heat, stirring all the time, bring the sauce to the boil so that it thickens. Stir in the egg yolks and cook them for a minute. Season the sauce and leave to cool slightly.

Dissolve the gelatine in the lemon juice then stir it into the sauce. Flake the salmon, removing any bones and skin, then stir it into the mixture with the cream, Drambuie, Tabasco sauce, mace and extra salt and pepper. Leave the mixture until it is nearly setting.

Whisk the egg white until stiff, fold a tablespoon into the soufflé mixture then lightly fold in the rest. Pour the mixture into the dish: it should come at least 1 inch above the edge. Leave overnight to set.

Next day carefully peel off the collar and serve the soufflé garnished with sliced cucumber.

Smoked Salmon

The method of curing is sometimes known as kippering salmon. It involves cutting the fish in half lengthways and removing the backbone. The fish is then salted for twenty-four hours, drained and left to drip for six hours, smothered with olive oil and left for another six hours, carefully drained again and rubbed with a cloth, then covered with demerara sugar and left as for the salt. Again the fish is hung to drain then treated with olive oil once more, wiped off with the cloth and finally smoked over the embers of a peat fire.

It is not surprising with such a time-consuming process that smoked salmon is considered a great delicacy.

For me it should simply be served in very thin slices and accompanied by lemon wedges and thinly sliced bread and butter.

Allow 1½–2 oz per person.

Facing page: Raised Game Pie

Left: Scottish cheeses: Crowdie; Orkney; Dunlop; Caboc and Oatcakes

Smoked Salmon Pâté

If you are fortunate enough to obtain from your fishmonger the trimmings from a side of smoked salmon or some inexpensive pieces, this is a delicious way of using them.

8 oz smoked salmon

2 oz soft butter (¼ cup)

1 tablespoon oil

1 tablespoon lemon juice

3 fl oz double cream (3½ tablespoons)

a pinch of nutmeg

freshly ground black pepper

Remove the skin and any small bones from the salmon, then mince or chop it finely.

Beat the butter and oil together until soft, then gradually beat in the fish until the mixture becomes thick. Mix in the lemon juice, cream, nutmeg and black pepper to taste then turn the pâté into a small dish and chill before serving with toast.

Trout with Almonds

Serves 4

4 rainbow trout, cleaned but with the heads left on

2 level tablespoons plain flour seasoned with salt and pepper

3 oz butter (6 tablespoons)

1 tablespoon corn oil

2 oz flaked almonds (½ cup)

the juice of half a lemon

Wash and thoroughly dry the trout, then toss them in the flour. Melt the oil and 1 oz (2 tablespoons) of the butter in a pan and fry the fish two at a time for about 5 minutes on each side, turning them very carefully. Drain the trout when cooked and keep them warm.

When all the fish are ready, wipe the pan clean then melt the rest of the butter and fry the almonds until brown. Remove the pan from the heat and stir in the lemon juice, then spoon the mixture over the fish before serving.

Trout Drambuie

Serves 4

4 rainbow trout, cleaned but with the heads left on

2 oz soft butter (¼ cup)

1 level teaspoon dried oregano

¼ pint natural yogurt (⅔ cup)

¼ pint double cream (⅔ cup)

1 tablespoon Drambuie

salt and pepper

Wash and thoroughly dry the fish. Spread an ovenproof dish with half the butter. Put the fish in the dish and spread them with the rest of the fat. Sprinkle over the oregano.

Mix the yogurt, cream and Drambuie together then season the mixture before pouring it over the trout. Bake the fish, uncovered, at Gas 4/350°F/180°C for 20 minutes. Garnish with lemon twists before serving.

Facing page: Fishing the 'Falls Pool' on the River Orkaig near Lochinvar

Poached Prawns Isle of May

Serves 6–8
2 lb peeled Scampi prawns
4 oz mushrooms, sliced (1 cup)
1 onion, finely chopped
½ pint white wine (1¼ cups)
2 oz butter (¼ cup)
2 oz plain flour (½ cup)
1 wineglass dry sherry
¼ pint double cream (⅔ cup)
salt and pepper
2 lb potatoes, boiled and mashed

This is a recipe from the Crusoe Hotel in Lower Largo in Fife. Lower Largo, a fine old Scottish seaside village, was the birthplace of Alexander Selkirk, whose experiences were the inspiration of Daniel Defoe's *Robinson Crusoe*. The Crusoe Hotel is run by Crawford and Hazel Horne and specializes in seafood. Here is one of its specialities.

Place the prawns, mushrooms, onion and white wine in a saucepan, cover and poach for about 10 to 15 minutes. Strain, reserving the liquor.

In another saucepan melt the butter, stir in the flour and cook for a few minutes without browning. Add the fish liquor and sherry, correcting the consistency with milk if it is too thick. Add the prawns, mushrooms and onion. Check the seasoning and lightly stir in the double cream. Reheat gently and serve in scallop shells, surrounded by a border of piped potato.

Prawns Eilean a'Chèo

Serves 1 as a main course or 2 as a starter
1 oz butter (2 tablespoons)
6 oz peeled raw prawns (scampi would do) (1 cup)
2 oz onion, finely chopped
2 oz fresh white mushrooms, sliced (½ cup)
¼ red pepper, finely chopped
salt and pepper
1 measure Drambuie
2 fl oz double cream (¼ cup)
2 oz long grain rice (4 tablespoons)
1 lemon, cut in wedges
parsley sprigs, to decorate
a few king prawns, to decorate

This recipe comes from the Post House Hotel in Aviemore. Aviemore, in the heart of the Highlands, is the well-known Spey Valley resort, with ski-ing and curling in winter and fishing, walking, riding and shooting in summer. Albert McKay is chef at the Post House Hotel, and has developed this recipe as a tribute to his home, the Island of Skye.

Boil the rice in plenty of salted water until cooked. Meanwhile melt the butter and sauté the prawns, onions and peppers. When the onions are almost cooked add the mushrooms and Drambuie. Season and add the cream. Serve on a bed of rice, topped with king prawns, lemon wedges and parsley sprigs.

Roast Beef

Scottish sirloin with its succulent undercut must be the king of all joints. Personally I think it is best cooked on the bone, but if you prefer the joint can be bought boned and rolled. Other beef joints suitable for roasting are wing rib (rib roast), a slightly smaller joint but excellent value for money, and top side (top round), which is usually bought already rolled.

Allow 20 minutes for every pound plus an extra 20 minutes for a medium roasted joint of beef. If the meat is to be rare allow only 15 minutes to the pound, or if well done, 25 minutes to the pound. The extra 20 minutes remains the same for all methods. Prick the surface of the fat with a fork and sprinkle it liberally with salt – this helps to give the meat a crispy surface. Melt 2–3 tablespoons of dripping in a roasting tin, add the joint fat side up so that the fat automatically bastes the meat. Cook at Gas 6/400°F/200°C for the first 20 minutes then lower the heat to Gas 5/375°F/190°C for the rest of the calculated cooking time. Leave a large joint to stand for 15 minutes in a warm place before carving.

Horseradish Sauce

4 level tablespoons grated fresh horseradish

½ level teaspoon mustard powder

1 dessertspoon wine vinegar (2 teaspoons)

1 level teaspoon caster sugar

¼ pint double cream (⅔ cup)

This creamy sauce, which is the traditional accompaniment to roast beef, is also delicious served with plain grilled trout or mackerel.

Mix the horseradish, mustard, vinegar, sugar and seasoning together. Whip the cream until it starts to hold its shape then stir in the other ingredients and serve the sauce in a small bowl.

Castle Stuart Steak

Serves 1

8–10 oz rump steak

1 oz butter (2 tablespoons)

1 tablespoon oil

2 tomatoes, peeled and deseeded

1 clove garlic, crushed

2 oz onion, finely chopped

salt and pepper

For the pâté

2 oz Castle Stuart Blue Cheese

2 oz butter ($\frac{1}{4}$ cup)

$\frac{1}{2}$ clove garlic, crushed

1 level dessertspoon onion, finely chopped (2 teaspoons)

a few drops of Worcester sauce

a few drops of lemon juice

This is another recipe from the Post House Hotel in Aviemore and is a truly sumptuous way of serving prime Scotch rump steak. If you cannot obtain the Castle Stuart cheese, Stilton may be used instead.

Make the pâté in advance by mixing all the ingredients together to form a creamy substance. Roll into greaseproof paper and chill.

Fry the steak on both sides in the butter and oil until it is done to your liking. Remove from the pan, keep warm, and add the garlic, onion and tomato to the pan juices, frying gently for a few moments until cooked. Put this on top of the steak, top with the pâté and melt under the grill.

Lowland Lamb

This recipe is based on an old-fashioned dish called Parson's or Friar's Venison.

Serves 6–8

a 4–4$\frac{1}{2}$ lb shoulder of lamb, boned

$\frac{1}{2}$ oz dripping (1 tablespoon)

$\frac{1}{4}$ pint stock ($\frac{2}{3}$ cup)

For the stuffing

4 oz ham, chopped ($\frac{2}{3}$ cup)

4 oz mushrooms (1 cup)

1 oz butter (2 tablespoons)

1 level tablespoon chopped chives

salt and pepper

For the marinade

$\frac{1}{4}$ pint red wine ($\frac{2}{3}$ cup)

6 juniper berries, chopped

$\frac{1}{4}$ level teaspoon ground allspice

2 tablespoons oil

2 tablespoons malt vinegar

1 bay leaf

$\frac{1}{4}$ level teaspoon ground nutmeg

Wipe, trim and chop the mushrooms, then sauté them in the butter until all of it has been absorbed, stir in the ham, chives and seasoning and leave to cool.

Season the inside of the boned lamb and when the stuffing is quite cold put it inside and sew up the joint to enclose the stuffing securely.

Mix the wine with the juniper berries, allspice, oil, vinegar, bay leaf and ground nutmeg and put it in a shallow china dish. Add the joint, turn it in the marinade to coat it, then loosely cover the meat and leave it at room temperature for about 12 hours while the flavours penetrate. Turn the meat once or twice during this time.

Next day melt the dripping in a roasting tin, add the drained joint and brown it well on both sides. Pour in the marinade and bring it to the boil, then cover the tin and roast the joint for 1$\frac{3}{4}$–2 hours at Gas 4/350°F/180°C or until the meat is tender. Baste it once or twice during cooking.

Dish the meat when cooked, skim off the fat from the surface of the liquid in the tin, then pour in the stock. Bring the sauce to the boil then strain it into a warm gravy boat for serving.

Roast Lamb

Scottish lamb is very tender and sweet and makes an excellent meat to roast. Suitable joints are leg, shoulder or best end of neck (rack), chined by the butcher.

Allow 20 minutes for every pound and add an extra 20 minutes to the total time. Wipe the joint then rub the surface with a cut clove of garlic and sprinkle it liberally with salt.

Melt 2 tablespoons of dripping in a tin, add the joint and cook the meat at Gas 6/400°F/200°C for the first 20 minutes, then reduce the heat to Gas 4/350°F/180°C for the rest of the calculated time, basting the meat twice during this time.

When the meat is cooked lift it onto a serving plate and allow it to rest in a warm place for 15 minutes to make it easier to carve. Use the sediment in the tin as a basis for the gravy, and accompany the meat with mint sauce or red currant jelly.

Sunday Lamb

This recipe is based on an old receipt published in the nineteenth century.

Serves 6

a shoulder of lamb

1 oz lard or dripping (2 tablespoons)

$\frac{1}{2}$ pint red wine ($1\frac{1}{4}$ cups)

$\frac{1}{2}$ pint stock ($1\frac{1}{4}$ cups)

$\frac{1}{2}$ teaspoon anchovy essence

1 teaspoon mushroom ketchup

salt, pepper and cayenne pepper

Weigh the joint and calculate the cooking time at 20 minutes to the pound plus 20 minutes.

Heat the lard and baste the lamb, then stand it on a rack and cook the joint at Gas 4/350°F/180°C for half the calculated cooking time.

Warm the wine, stock, anchovy essence, mushroom ketchup and seasoning together. Drain the fat from the meat then pour over the sauce. Baste the joint and return it to the oven to complete the cooking time. Baste the joint several more times during the cooking so that it really absorbs the flavour of the sauce.

Serve the joint with roast potatoes.

Gigot Lamb Chops and Ginger Sauce

Serves 4

4 gigot (leg) lamb chops

4 dessertspoons lime jelly
marmalade (3 tablespoons)

For the sauce

2 tablespoons soft brown sugar

2 tablespoons wine vinegar

1 tablespoon lemon juice

1 teaspoon ground ginger

a little cornflour

This recipe comes from the Beechwood Country House Hotel, Moffat. Moffat is a market town in Annandale with strong wool trade connections. It lies just south of the Grey Mares' Tails waterfall and the Devil's Beef Tub, an enormous natural hollow used during border skirmishes to hide rustled cattle.

Mrs Jessie Anderson runs the Beechwood Country House Hotel which overlooks the town. She does all the cooking herself, using Scottish ingredients with great ingenuity to produce subtle and original dishes.

Place the chops in a baking dish and put a dessertspoonful of jelly marmalade on each. Mix together all the sauce ingredients except the cornflour and pour over the chops. Allow to soak for at least one hour.

Cover with foil and bake for an hour at Gas 4/350°F/180°C. Before serving thicken the sauce slightly with a little cornflour mixed to a paste with cold water.

Black-faced sheep above the Edenbon Burn, Forest of Atholl, Perthshire

Glorious Game

Scotland is the home of game, and nowadays all sorts are readily available to roast, casserole, bake in a pie or boil in a pudding. Each variety has its own season, but shooting begins on the glorious 12th of August with grouse and goes through the winter until the breeding season in March.

After being shot most game should be hung to develop the flavour and tenderize the meat. The length of hanging time depends on the weather and on personal taste, but ranges from three days to ten. Water birds such as teal and wild duck require less time and should only be hung for one to two days. The birds are not plucked before being hung and are ready for cooking when the tail feathers pluck out easily and the thin flesh over the abdomen is slightly green in colour.

When hanging time is complete the birds are plucked, drawn and trussed ready for cooking. Young succulent birds are best roasted and the older and drier ones reserved for casseroling. Young birds have soft, pliable feet and the tip of the breast bone is also pliable; they will have soft, downy plumage on the breast, pointed wings, again with soft downy plumage underneath, and rounded spurs. Older birds have hard, scaly feet and the claws of pheasant or grouse are sharp.

Partridge

Season: 1 September to 1 February

Young, tender partridge are hung for up to a week and are best roasted in the same way as grouse. Either fill the centre with butter or follow the gypsy method and use wild mushrooms.

Allow one small or half a large partridge per person, splitting it straight down the centre once cooked. Bake as for grouse at Gas 6/400°F/200°C for 30–45 minutes, depending on size, and serve with Baked Apples and Fried Breadcrumbs (see Accompaniments, pages 143 and 139). Watercress and lemon wedges complete the dish.

Grouse

Season: 12 August to 10 December

There are four types of grouse: wood grouse (capercailzie), black grouse, red grouse and white grouse (ptarmigan). Of the four the red grouse is considered the most succulent. It should weigh just over 1 pound and be hung for three to ten days, depending on the age of the bird.

As you see for this recipe I have suggested placing butter in the carcasses of the birds to keep them moist. Some cooks advocate the addition of red whortleberries or cranberries from the bird's native moorland.

Serves 4

2 grouse (preferably hen birds)

2 oz butter ($\frac{1}{4}$ cup)

4 rashers streaky bacon

a squeeze of lemon juice

salt and pepper

flour

2 slices of toast

Knead the lemon juice into the butter with seasoning. Wipe the birds inside and out (do not wash them). Divide the butter between the birds, putting a piece inside each. Wrap the bacon over the breast, place the birds in a tin and roast them at Gas 6/400 F/200 C for half to three-quarters of an hour, basting occasionally with more butter. About 10 minutes before the end of the cooking time remove the bacon, baste the birds again, dust with flour and return to the oven to complete cooking. The birds should be just cooked, in other words still slightly pink at the joints.

Lightly fry the grouse livers in butter then mash them and spread them onto the slices of toast. Remove the string from the birds and place one on each slice of toast. Garnish with watercress and serve with game chips, bread sauce and fried breadcrumbs (see Accompaniments, page 139).

*Black Grouse:
an early print
by Ackermann*

Pheasant

Season: 15 October to 1 February

Pheasant are often bought by the brace, which is a cock and a hen bird. The hen bird usually has more flavour and is less dry than the cock. The birds are hung for up to ten days and each one should feed about three people.

Serves 6

a brace of pheasants

6 oz streaky bacon rashers

6 oz fresh white breadcrumbs (1¼ cups)

4 oz melted butter (½ cup)

Wipe the birds inside and out. Stir the breadcrumbs into the melted butter then divide the mixture between the birds, packing it into the carcass of each. Re-tie the pheasants and then place them in a roasting tin. Cover each with the bacon, making sure the breasts are well protected.

Cook the birds at Gas 6/400°F/200°C for 10 minutes, reduce the heat to Gas 4/350°F/180°C and cook for a further 40–50 minutes. About 10 minutes before the end of the cooking time, remove the bacon so that the birds can brown.

Serve the pheasants adorned with their tail feathers and watercress and accompanied by game chips and bread sauce (see Accompaniments, page 139).

Scots Pheasant

Serves 3

a large pheasant, oven ready

4 oz butter (½ cup)

2 lb Cox's eating apples, peeled, cored and sliced (6 cups)

¼ pint single cream (⅔ cup)

2 fl oz Drambuie (¼ cup)

salt and pepper

Wipe the pheasant. Melt half the butter in a pan, add the bird and brown it on all sides. Transfer to a plate. Melt the rest of the butter, add the apples and cook until they start to colour. Turn half into a small casserole dish, put the pheasant in breast down, then arrange the remaining apple round the bird. Pour over half the cream and cook the casserole covered at Gas 4/350°F/180°C for 1¼ hours, turning the bird half way through the cooking time.

Remove the dish from the oven and increase the heat to Gas 8/450°F/220°C, pour the Drambuie and remaining cream over the bird, adjust the mixture for seasoning then cover the dish again and return it to the oven for 5–10 minutes to complete the cooking.

Venison

Season: theoretically venison is in season from June to the end of September for bucks and October to December for does, although it is very unusual to see venison in the shops before October. The late autumn and winter are the best months as the animal has had time to put on some fat.

Venison can tend to be very dry when roasted so it is best to marinade the joint first. It should be hung for seven to ten days to improve the flavour and is ready when it smells quite high and gamey. Cuts for roasting are best taken from the haunch, which is the loin and leg.

Roast Haunch of Venison

Serves 4–6

a 2–2½ lb haunch of venison

4 oz dripping or butter (½ cup)

For the marinade

½ pint red wine (1¼ cups)

2 tablespoons vinegar

4 tablespoons cooking oil

1 carrot, peeled and sliced

1 onion, peeled and sliced

3 sprigs of parsley

6 crushed peppercorns

4 juniper berries

For the sauce

¼ pint soured cream (⅔ cup)

1 tablespoon French mustard

¼ pint stock (⅔ cup)

Wipe the surface of the meat. In a deep casserole mix the wine, vinegar and oil together then stir in the carrot, onion, parsley, peppercorns and juniper berries. Add the venison and baste it with the marinade, then leave the pot in a cool place loosely covered for 12–24 hours, basting the meat occasionally.

Remove the venison from the marinade and wipe it dry. Place the meat in a roasting tin and cover it thickly with the dripping or butter. Strain the marinade and pour half of it into the tin. Then cover the tin with foil and roast the joint at Gas 4/350°F/180°C for 25 minutes to the pound plus 25 minutes. Half an hour before the end of the cooking time remove the foil from the tin, baste the joint and increase the heat to Gas 6/400°F/200°C.

When the joint is cooked lift it onto an ashet and leave in a warm place. Skim the fat from the surface of the juice in the tin. Add the rest of the strained marinade and the stock and bring the liquid to the boil. Mix the soured cream with the mustard, pour in a little of the hot liquid and when it is blended return it to the rest of the liquid. Heat but do not boil, or the sauce will curdle. Check for seasoning before serving with redcurrant or rowan jelly.

Casseroled Venison Macduff

Serves 6

2 lb lean venison (boned haunch)

4 oz butter ($\frac{1}{2}$ cup)

4 oz flour (1 cup)

2 onions

8 oz mushrooms (2 cups)

$\frac{1}{4}$ lb diced bacon

$\frac{1}{2}$ pint red wine or port ($1\frac{1}{4}$ cups)

1 small tin cranberries

$\frac{1}{4}$ teaspoon cinnamon

$\frac{1}{4}$ teaspoon nutmeg

salt and pepper

A deliciously rich-flavoured venison casserole from the Crusoe Hotel in Fife. The sharp, fruity cranberries from its native moors are the perfect complement to the venison.

Dice the venison and sauté in the butter until lightly coloured. Add the spices, seasoning, bacon and onions and sauté a further 2 minutes. Add the flour, adding more if necessary to absorb all the fat. Add the wine or port and bring to the boil. Correct the consistency with stock or extra wine if necessary. Add the mushrooms and cranberries, check the seasoning, cover and simmer for 2–2$\frac{1}{2}$ hours, preferably in a slow oven, Gas 2/300°F/150°C.

Serve with green noodles.

Wild Duck

Season: all the year round but best between September and February.

Wild duck tends to have a fishy taste, so before cooking it is best to place the prepared bird in a roasting tin and pour in boiling salted water to a depth of half an inch. Roast the bird for 10 minutes at Gas 4/350°F/180°C, basting it frequently. Drain.

Place the bird in a dry roasting tin, put a bunch of parsley, a nut of butter and the duck liver into the carcass, pour over a little melted butter and cover the breast with bacon. Roast at Gas 4/350°F/180°C for 20–30 minutes, basting frequently and removing the bacon for the last 10 minutes. Dust the bird with flour and baste yet again before returning it to the oven to complete the cooking time. Wild duck should be served slightly pink. Use the juices in the pan to make a thin gravy and serve the duck with an orange salad or Spiced Plums (see pages 143 and 140).

Jugged Hare

Serves 6

1 hare paunched and jointed by the butcher (ask for the blood too)

2 oz dripping (¼ cup)

2 medium onions, peeled and each stuck with a clove

6 peppercorns

1 bay leaf

a sprig of thyme

a sprig of parsley

1 level teaspoon allspice berries

3 medium carrots, peeled and quartered

1 stick celery, washed and chopped

the juice of 1 lemon

1½–2 pints stock (4–5 cups)

salt

2 level tablespoons flour

For the thickening

the hare's blood or stock

2 level dessertspoons cornflour (5 teaspoons)

2 level tablespoons redcurrant jelly

salt and pepper

1 tablespoon port

For the stuffing balls

4 oz fresh breadcrumbs (¾ cup)

2 level tablespoons prepared shredded suet

1 medium onion, peeled and finely chopped

1 level tablespoon chopped parsley

1 bacon rasher

2 standard eggs (size 3), beaten

dry white breadcrumbs

deep fat for frying

Hare has been a popular meat for many centuries, and this famous recipe takes its name from the early cooking method. The hare was jointed, packed into a jug or 7-pound pickle jar with seasoning and no liquid other than its own blood, and the container was placed inside a larger one of boiling water.

Soak the joints of hare in cold salted water for 2–3 hours, then drain and dry them. Cut the leg joints in half. Melt the dripping in a frying pan and fry the joints until brown on either side. Transfer them to a large casserole dish. Add the onions, peppercorns, bay leaf, thyme, parsley, allspice berries, carrots, celery and lemon juice and a good pinch of salt. Pour in the stock, cover the dish and seal the lid with a flour and water paste. Bake the hare at Gas 4/350°F/180°C for 1 hour, then reduce the heat to Gas 2/300°F/150°C and cook for a further 2 hours or until the hare is really tender.

To make the stuffing balls

Cut the rind from the bacon then chop the rasher finely. Fry it until crisp. Mix together the fresh breadcrumbs, suet, chopped onion, parsley, bacon and seasoning. Bind the mixture with half the beaten egg, then roll it into small balls. Brush the balls with the rest of the egg then toss them in the breadcrumbs.

Heat the deep fat until a cube of bread starts to brown immediately it is immersed in it. Put the stuffing balls into the basket and lower them into the fat for about 2 minutes or until golden brown. Drain and keep warm.

To complete the dish

Lift the pieces of hare onto a serving dish and strain the juices from the casserole dish into a pan. Blend the cornflour with the hare's blood, add a little gravy to this then stir it back into the liquid. Mix in the redcurrant jelly then, stirring constantly, bring the gravy to the boil. Add the port wine and check for seasoning. Then pour the gravy over the hare and garnish the dish with the stuffing balls. Serve with redcurrant jelly and racks of dry toast.

Raised Game Pie

Serves 6

6 oz grouse cut into 1-inch pieces

6 oz hare cut into 1-inch pieces

1 lb belly of pork

2 tablespoons red wine

1 level teaspoon ground nutmeg

salt and pepper

8 oz streaky bacon rashers

1 level teaspoon mixed herbs

$\frac{1}{4}$–$\frac{1}{2}$ pint aspic jelly ($\frac{2}{3}$–$1\frac{1}{4}$ cups)

For the pastry

1 lb plain flour ($3\frac{1}{2}$–4 cups)

5 oz lard (10 tablespoons)

$1\frac{1}{4}$ level teaspoons salt

$\frac{1}{2}$ pint water ($1\frac{1}{4}$ cups)

a little beaten egg for glaze

Mix the grouse and hare with the wine and half the herbs and nutmeg and leave the mixture to marinade.

Cut the skin and any bones from the pork and mince it coarsely with two of the bacon rashers, then stir in the rest of the seasoning.

Sift the flour and salt for the pastry into a bowl. Melt the lard over a low heat then add the water and bring the liquid to the boil. Immediately pour it into the flour and using a fork mix the ingredients together to form a soft dough. Using three-quarters of it line the base and sides of either an 8-inch raised pie mould or a 6-inch round cake tin, so that they are evenly covered and the pastry extends just over the rim. Keep the dough for the lid covered with the mixing bowl to keep it warm and pliable.

Remove the rind and any bones from the rest of the bacon and line the pastry lining with it. Pack half the pork in the bottom then add the game and then the remaining pork.

Cover the pie with the pastry for the lid, sealing the edges really well together, decorate the top of the pie and make a hole to release the steam as the pie cooks.

Glaze the pastry with egg. Bake at Gas 6/400°F/200°C for 30 minutes then reduce the heat to Gas 3/325°F/160°C and cook for a further 1–$1\frac{1}{2}$ hours or until golden brown.

Leave the pie to cool. Next day dissolve the aspic jelly and leave it until quite cold and just on the point of setting. Make a hole in the centre of the pie, pour in the jelly to fill the gaps around the meat and leave it to set. Serve game pie for a picnic with a salad.

Accompaniments for Game

Serve a selection of these side dishes with roast game birds. Skirlie (see page 73) is also served with grouse and pheasant.

Game Chips

I must confess that sometimes when serving game chips I cheat and buy plain potato crisps and heat them up in the oven for a few minutes. However, here is how to make game chips correctly.

Serves 6
1 lb potatoes, peeled
deep fat for frying

Using a potato peeler or mandoline, slice the potatoes wafer thin. Put the slices into a bowl of iced water and leave them until required.

Drain the slices and dry them thoroughly. Heat a deep fat fryer half full of oil to 375°F/190°C and fry the chips, a few at a time, until golden brown. Drain on kitchen paper and keep warm while the rest are being cooked. Sprinkle with salt before serving.

Fried Breadcrumbs

4 oz fresh white breadcrumbs
(¾ cup)
1–2 oz butter (2–4 tablespoons)

Melt the butter in a pan, add the crumbs and fry them over a low heat, stirring all the time until the butter is absorbed. Increase the heat and fry the crumbs until they are evenly brown.

Bread Sauce

This is one of the few sauces which can claim to have originated in Scotland.

Serves 6
¾ pint milk (2 cups)
1 onion, peeled and stuck with 6 cloves
4 oz stale bread, crusts removed
salt and pepper
1 bay leaf
1 oz butter (2 tablespoons)
a pinch of nutmeg

Place the clove-studded onion in a pan with the bay leaf and the milk. Heat the ingredients together so that the milk absorbs the flavours. Then stir in the bread cut into pieces and leave the sauce on one side to soak for an hour.

Return the pan to the heat and bring it back to the boil, remove the onion and cloves and the bay leaf and beat the sauce with a fork until smooth. Stir in the butter, nutmeg and seasoning and pour the sauce into a warm dish for serving.

Spiced Plums

These plums are a marvellous preserve to have in the store cupboard. Not only do they make a delicious accompaniment to duck, but they are also perfect served as an instant dessert with junket.

3 lb plums

the grated rind and juice of 1 orange and 1 lemon

3 lb granulated sugar (6 cups)

6 cloves

3-inch piece of cinnamon stick

3 tablespoons Drambuie

Wipe, halve and stone the plums. Place them in a bowl in layers with the sugar and grated orange and lemon rind. Sprinkle over the juices then leave the bowl, covered with a cloth, in a cool place overnight.

Next day transfer the fruit to a large casserole dish with all the juice and undissolved sugar. Add the cloves and cinnamon stick, put on the lid then bake the plums at the bottom of the oven at Gas 1/275°F/140°C for 4 hours. When the plums are cooked leave them to cool in the dish.

Stir in the Drambuie, remove the cloves and cinnamon and store the fruit in screw-topped jars (I usually use Kilner jars) in a cool, dry, dark place for about 3 months before serving.

Rowan Jelly

Rowan berries are the scarlet fruit clusters of the mountain ash tree. The jelly is served with mountain mutton and game, while redcurrant jelly is served with valley meat.

Makes about 4 lb

2 lb rowans

1 lb crab apples

2 pints water (5 cups)

granulated sugar

Wash the berries, remove any damaged ones, and snip off the excess stalks. Put the fruit into a pan with the apples, roughly chopped. Add the water then simmer the fruits until soft – about 30 minutes. Strain the liquid through a scalded jelly bag and leave it overnight to drip – do not be tempted to squeeze the bag or a cloudy jelly will result.

Next day measure the liquid and add 1 lb sugar to every pint of juice (2 cups per 2½ cups liquid). Gradually dissolve the sugar in the syrup then bring the jelly to the boil and boil it until setting point – about 15 minutes. Test for set as in Apricot Jam, page 101. Put into warm clean jars, cover, label and store until required.

Facing page: Scottish Royal Pancakes

Redcurrant Jelly

Makes about 5 lb
4 lb redcurrants (13 cups)
about 2 pints cold water (5 cups)
granulated sugar

Wash the fruit and put it into a pan still on the stalks. Add enough water to come level with the fruit. Bring the liquid to the boil, then reduce the heat and simmer the redcurrants covered for about 30 minutes or until they are really soft.

Continue as for Rowan Jelly. This jelly will take about 5 minutes to reach setting point.

Baked Apples

Allow 1 eating apple per person. Cut out the cores and place in a small roasting tin. Fill the centres with redcurrant jelly and bake on the shelf under the game for about 20 minutes or until just soft. Fill the centres with more redcurrant jelly after the apples have been placed round the meat for serving.

Orange Salad

This is an excellent complement to wild duck, its sharp fruitiness contrasting beautifully with the rich meat.

Allow 1 orange per person. Using a potato peeler pare the rind only from the oranges then cut it into needle-thin strips and place them in a pan. Cover with cold water, bring to the boil and cook for 3 minutes, drain and run under cold water to refresh.

With a sharp knife remove all the pith from the fruit and slice the oranges thinly. Arrange them on a serving dish, sprinkle with sugar and black pepper and pour over a well flavoured French dressing. Leave the salad in a cool place to marinade for 2 hours then sprinkle over the orange shreds before serving.

Left: Summer Pudding with raspberries and Drambuie Cream

Atholl Brose Pudding

Serves 4

½ pint double cream (1¼ cups)

3 fl oz whisky (¼ cup)

3 tablespoons runny heather honey

2 oz pinhead oatmeal, toasted (⅓ cup)

Although traditionally Atholl Brose is served as a drink (see page 170), with the addition of cream it can become a very extravagant dessert.

Whip the cream until it just holds its shape. Stir in the oatmeal with the honey. Chill, then just before serving mix in the whisky. Serve in small stemmed glasses.

Cranachan

Serves 4

3 oz pinhead oatmeal (½ cup)

½ pint double cream (1¼ cups)

1 tablespoon Drambuie (optional)

This dessert is also sometimes known as Cream Crowdie.

Toast the oatmeal in a frying pan over a fairly high heat until it is lightly browned. Sift out any dust.

Whisk the cream to a soft consistency, then mix in the Drambuie and toasted oatmeal. Serve in glasses.

A favourite way of mine to make the dessert extra special is to fold in about 6 oz (1½ cups) of Scottish raspberries.

Orange Whisky Cream

Serves 6

1 packet orange jelly

¾ pint double cream (2 cups)

5 tablespoons thick orange marmalade

2 tablespoons whisky

2 teaspoons powdered gelatine

This recipe was devised by Mrs Anderson of the Beechwood Country House Hotel.

Make up the jelly with ¾ pint boiling water. Pour ½ pint of the jelly into a bowl and, stirring well, add the gelatine. Chill quickly to a sloppy consistency, but do not allow to set firm.

To the remaining ¼ pint jelly add the whisky and cool at room temperature.

Whip the cream, but not stiffly. Add the marmalade, mix in well, and stir this into the ½ pint of half-set jelly.

Pour half this mixture into a dish and set rapidly in the freezer. When set pour on, very carefully, the ¼ pint of whisky-flavoured jelly. Again, set rapidly in the freezer. Pour on the rest of the cream and set in the refrigerator.

Grosert Fool

This rich fool, made with Scotland's native gooseberry and plenty of double cream, can be frozen to make a delicious ice cream. A more economical version for family puddings can be made using half cream and half custard.

Serves 4

1 lb gooseberries, topped and tailed (3¼ cups)

4–6 oz sugar (½–¾ cup)

½ pint double dream (1¼ cups)

green food colouring (optional)

Wash the gooseberries and drain well. Put them into a pan and simmer over a low heat until tender. Rub the fruit through a nylon sieve to make a purée, then stir in enough sugar to sweeten. Colour the purée with a little green food colouring, if it is very pale, and leave it on one side to cool.

Whip the cream until it holds its shape, fold in the cold purée, then turn it into a dish to chill for several hours.

Serve with sponge fingers or shortbread biscuits.

A Burnt Cream

Although this famous recipe is now associated with Trinity College, Cambridge, it originated in a country house in Scotland during the nineteenth century.

Heat the double cream to just below boiling point. Beat the egg yolks and the 3 tablespoons of sugar together then slowly beat in the cream with the vanilla essence.

Strain the liquid into a 1½-pint shallow ovenproof dish. Stand it in a roasting tin with hot water coming half way up the sides, then cover the surface with a sheet of greaseproof paper. Cook the custard at Gas 4/350°F/180°C for 40 minutes or until it is lightly set. Leave to cool overnight.

To complete the dessert sprinkle the surface thickly with caster sugar and place the dish under a pre-heated grill for a few seconds so that the sugar melts and caramelizes.

Leave to cool and harden before serving with fresh raspberries.

Serves 6

1 pint double cream (2½ cups)

4 large egg yolks (size 2)

3 level tablespoons caster sugar

a drop of vanilla essence

extra caster sugar for the top

Drambuie Cream

Serves 6–8

¾ pint milk (2 cups)

3 oz caster sugar (⅓ cup)

½ oz powdered gelatine
(2 US envelopes)

2 tablespoons cold water

2 large eggs (size 2)

½ pint double cream (1¼ cups)

4 fl oz Drambuie (½ cup)

8 oz Scottish raspberries, to
decorate

Heat the milk to just below boiling point. Beat the eggs and sugar together, then stir in a little of the milk. When the mixture is smooth return it to the milk in the pan and, stirring all the time, over a medium heat, cook the custard until it thickens. Do not allow it to boil. Set the pan on one side to cool.

Soak the gelatine in the cold water for about 10 minutes and when it has become a solid mass stir it into the hot custard a bit at a time so that it dissolves. Leave the custard until it starts to set.

Whisk the cream to the same consistency as the custard, whisk in the Drambuie, then fold the two mixtures together. Turn the whole into a lightly greased 2-pint mould and leave overnight to set.

Next day turn the Drambuie Cream onto a dish and decorate with Scottish raspberries.

Hatted Kit

Serves 4–6

½ pint double cream (1¼ cups)

the grated rind and juice of 1
lemon

about ¼ pint white wine (⅔ cup)

4 oz caster sugar (½ cup)

There are many versions of this recipe, all varying slightly, but all requiring raw milk and/or buttermilk. This is obviously not very practical for everyone so I have adapted one Hatted Kit recipe called Syllabub Under the Cow into a syllabub suitable to make at home, and I feel sure you will enjoy it.

Make the lemon juice up to ¼ pint (⅔ cup) with white wine, stir in the sugar and lemon rind and leave the mixture covered overnight in a cool place.

Next day whisk the cream and as it starts to thicken gradually whisk in the wine mixture to form a soft creamy consistency.

Serve within an hour of making and accompany the dessert with shortbread biscuits – or it is especially good with Scottish raspberries.

Typsy Laird

Serves 6–8

6 sponge cakes

½ lb raspberry jam (¾ cup)

the finely grated rind of 1 lemon

2 oz ratafia biscuits

¼ pint medium sweet sherry or fruit juice (⅔ cup)

2 tablespoons Drambuie

4 egg yolks

1 pint milk (2½ cups)

1 oz caster sugar (2 tablespoons)

a little vanilla essence

¼ pint double cream (⅔ cup)

flaked browned almonds, glacé cherries and angelica

a little extra Drambuie

This delicious pudding, also known as Scots Trifle, uses Scotland's own liqueur, Drambuie.

Split the sponges in half, spread them with jam and place them in a glass dish. Roughly crush the ratafia biscuits and scatter them on top with the lemon rind. Mix together the sherry and Drambuie, pour it over the sponges and leave to soak.

Beat the egg yolks and sugar together. Heat the milk to blood temperature and stir it into the egg yolks. When it is well blended return the liquid to the pan and, stirring all the time over a low heat, cook the custard until it thickens. Pour it into the dish and leave it to cool and set.

Next day, whisk the cream to a soft peak consistency and whisk in a little of the Drambuie. Turn the cream onto the trifle, ease it to the sides and decorate with the nuts, cherries and angelica.

Scottish Royal Pancakes

Serves 4

For the batter

4 oz plain flour (1 cup)

a pinch of salt

2 eggs, beaten

½ pint of milk (1¼ cups)

For the sauce

3 large oranges

2 large lemons

3 oz butter (6 tablespoons)

4 oz caster sugar (½ cup)

3 tablespoons Drambuie

Sieve the flour and salt into a bowl and make a well in the centre. Stir in the eggs and half the milk to make a smooth batter, then beat well. Gradually beat in the remaining milk.

Melt a little lard in an 8-inch frying pan and pour in enough batter to cover thinly the base of the pan. Fry until the underside is brown. Turn and cook until brown on the other side. Turn the pancake onto a tea towel, cover up and keep warm. Make seven more pancakes.

Grate the rinds from the oranges and lemons and then squeeze out the juice. Melt the butter in a frying pan, stir in the sugar and cook for one minute. Add the grated rinds, strain in the orange and lemon juices and bring to the boil. Add the Drambuie and simmer for 3 minutes.

Fold each pancake into quarters and place in the sauce. Simmer gently for 3 minutes, spooning sauce over the pancakes. Serve two pancakes for each person with a little sauce.

Heather Flan

Serves 6

For the base

6 oz crushed digestive biscuits

1 level dessertspoon caster sugar
(2 teaspoons)

1 oz chopped walnuts
(3 tablespoons)

½ level teaspoon cinnamon powder

3 oz butter, melted
(6 tablespoons)

For the filling

½ lb blaeberries or raspberries

¼ pint double cream (⅔ cup)

¼ pint soured cream (⅔ cup)

2 level dessertspoons caster sugar
(5 teaspoons)

If you cannot obtain blaeberries, do try this flan using the marvellous Scottish raspberries – it really is very good.

Stand a 7½-inch flan ring on a serving plate.

Mix the biscuit crumbs with the sugar, walnuts and cinnamon, stir in the melted butter and turn the mixture into the flan ring. Press it firmly and evenly over the base and up the sides and leave the case in a cool place for about an hour to chill.

Sprinkle some of the blaeberries over the base of the case. Whip the double cream until it stands in soft peaks, then stir in the soured cream and sugar and spoon the filling over the blaeberries. Scatter the rest of the fruit over the filling, carefully remove the ring and serve immediately.

Summer Pudding

Serves 4–6

8 thinly cut slices of stale bread

¼ lb redcurrants (1 cup)

1 lb raspberries (3¼ cups)

6 oz caster sugar (¾ cup)

½ pint water (1¼ cups)

This pudding is sometimes called Hydropathic Pudding because it was served to people unable to digest pastry.

Brush a 2-pint basin with a little oil. Remove the crust from the bread and line the base and sides of the basin with slices cut to fit. Keep some slices for the top.

Stalk the redcurrants and pick over the raspberries. Dissolve the sugar in the water and bring it to the boil. Add the fruit, bring it back to the boil, then remove the pan from the heat and leave the fruit to cook in the heat of the syrup.

Strain the fruit and pack half of it into the base of the lined dish, cover with a layer of bread then add the rest of the fruit and the final layer of bread. Pour in enough juice to soak into the bread but be careful not to make it too moist or it may not hold its shape. Keep the rest of the juice for later. Cover the pudding with a plate, weight it and leave overnight in a cool place.

Next day, thicken the remaining juice with arrowroot using about 1–2 teaspoons. Leave to cool. Turn the pudding out, pour over a little of the sauce and serve the rest in a sauce boat.

Drambuie Soufflé

Although this soufflé is delicious on its own or with single cream, try it with a melba sauce made from Scottish raspberries – you will find the combination superb.

Serves 4

4 large eggs (size 2), separated

1 oz butter (2 tablespoons)

1 oz plain flour ($\frac{1}{4}$ cup)

$\frac{1}{4}$ pint milk ($\frac{2}{3}$ cup)

3 oz caster sugar ($\frac{1}{3}$ cup)

4 tablespoons Drambuie

a few drops vanilla essence

Lightly butter a 2-pint soufflé dish and sprinkle it with caster sugar.

Melt the butter, stir in the flour, remove from the heat and gradually blend in the milk. When the sauce is smooth return it to the heat and bring it to the boil to thicken, stirring all the time. Stir in the egg yolks one at a time, then beat in the caster sugar with the Drambuie and vanilla essence.

Whisk the egg whites until they stand in soft peaks, then using a metal spoon lightly and quickly fold them into the sauce mixture.

Turn the soufflé into the dish and bake it in the middle of the oven at Gas 5/375°F/190°C for about 40 minutes or until it is well risen and golden brown.

Scatter a little icing sugar over the top then serve immediately.

Melba Sauce

1 lb fresh or frozen raspberries ($3\frac{1}{4}$ cups)

about 4 oz sifted icing sugar (1 cup)

Sieve the raspberries through a nylon sieve and gradually stir in sufficient icing sugar to taste.

Raspberry Soufflé

Serves 6

3 large eggs (size 2), separated

3 oz caster sugar (⅓ cup)

½ oz powdered gelatine
(2 US envelopes)

the juice of ½ lemon made up to 3
fl oz (6 tablespoons) with water

½ pint sieved raspberries (1¼ cups)

¼ pint double cream (⅔ cup)

1 oz chopped browned almonds
(3 tablespoons)

a few extra raspberries for
decoration

Encircle a 1¾-pint soufflé dish with a doubled sheet of foil that stands about 2 inches above the rim of the dish. Fasten it with tape.

Put the egg yolks and sugar into a bowl, suspend the bowl over a pan of hot water and whisk the mixture until it is thick and creamy in consistency. Remove the bowl from the heat.

Dissolve the gelatine in the lemon juice and water over a low heat, then beat it into the creamy mixture and continue beating until the mixture cools.

Whisk the cream to a soft peak consistency. Reserve a little for decoration then fold the rest into the mixture with the raspberry purée.

Stirring occasionally, leave the soufflé mixture until it is on the point of setting. Quickly whisk the egg whites until they are stiff, then fold them into the mixture and pour it into the soufflé dish. Leave the soufflé overnight to set.

To serve, remove the foil collar carefully with the help of a palette knife. Press the nuts into the soufflé mixture standing above the rim of the dish so that they adhere, then decorate with the remaining cream and extra raspberries.

Strawberry Water Ice

1 lb fresh strawberries (3¼ cups)

4 oz granulated sugar (½ cup)

4 tablespoons cold water

1 dessertspoon lemon juice (2
teaspoons)

1 dessertspoon orange juice (2
teaspoons)

Dissolve the sugar in the water in a pan over a low heat. When every grain has melted bring the syrup to the boil and boil it rapidly for 5 minutes. Remove the pan from the heat and leave the syrup on one side to cool.

Wash the strawberries, remove the stalks and rub the fruit through a nylon sieve to make a purée. Alternatively the fruit can be puréed in a liquidizer. Stir in the lemon and orange juice with the cold syrup. Pour this liquid into a shallow metal container and leave it overnight to freeze completely.

To serve, remove the water ice from the freezer and leave it at room temperature for 30 minutes to soften, then scoop it into individual glasses.

Prince Charles Pears

Serves 6

6 firm ripe pears

½ pint water (1¼ cups)

1 orange

4 oz soft brown sugar (½ cup, firmly packed)

2 level teaspoons arrowroot

4 tablespoons Drambuie

Using a potato peeler, remove the skin from the pears and as much of the core as possible, but leave the stalks in place.

Put the water and sugar into a shallow pan, and over a low heat dissolve the sugar, stirring occasionally. Pare the rind from the orange, again using the potato peeler, and add it to the pan with the orange juice. When the sugar has melted, bring the syrup to the boil. Then reduce the heat, add the pears, cover and poach them gently for about 40 minutes or until tender but still whole.

Transfer the pears to a serving dish. Remove the orange rind and cut about half of it into very fine strips to use for decoration.

Blend the arrowroot to a smooth consistency with the Drambuie, stir it into the syrup, then over a low heat and stirring all the time bring the sauce to the boil to thicken and clear.

Spoon the sauce over the pears and scatter with the orange shreds. Serve with single cream.

Drambuie Spiced Peaches

Serves 6

10 fresh peaches

4 tablespoons Drambuie

½ pint cold water (1¼ cups)

8 oz caster sugar (1 cup)

¼ level teaspoon nutmeg

a 2-inch piece of cinnamon stick

Put the water, sugar, nutmeg and cinnamon stick into a pan and over a very low heat dissolve the sugar. Then bring the syrup to the boil and boil it rapidly for a minute. Remove the pan from the heat.

Plunge the peaches into a pan of boiling water for a quick count of ten, then transfer them to cold water and peel off the skins. Cut each peach in half and remove the stone. Put the fruit halves into the syrup and poach them over a low heat for 3 minutes.

Leave the fruit in the syrup to cool then stir in the Drambuie and chill the peaches for at least 4 hours before serving.

Serve with single cream.

The Cheeses of Scotland

Although the Scottish cheeses are perhaps not so distinctive as the English or continental ones there are several that I think are worth mentioning.

Dunlop   Named after an Ayrshire parish, this cheese has an intriguing history. During the reign of Charles II a woman called Barbara Gilmour fled to Ireland to avoid persecution from the Covenanters. There she learned the art of making a sweet, unskimmed milk cheese, and on her return to Ayrshire in 1688 she introduced the skill. It soon became a profitable industry. Dunlop cheese can be purchased either red or white and is fairly similar to Cheddar, although the flavour is more mellow and the texture slightly softer. Dunlop can be used in cooking although I think it is better for eating.

Orkney   This cheese was the staple diet of the islanders. It was made in the crofts, usually with skimmed milk, and stored buried in tubs of oatmeal. Like Dunlop, Orkney cheese is a mild Cheddar and can be bought red or white. Some are smoked which gives the cheese a very delicate flavour.

Stewart   This is the Stilton of Scotland, although it does not have quite the same depth of flavour and character. The blue cheese is mild in taste and can be used in cooking quite successfully. The white cheese tends to be rather salty.

Caboc   My favourite Scottish cheese, Caboc, was first made in the Highlands in the fifteenth century, and the recipe has been handed down through one family. It is a full cream cheese shaped like a cork and rolled in oatmeal to give it a nutty taste and texture.

Hramsa   Another cheese originating from the Highlands, Hramsa is a soft curd cheese flavoured with herbs and garlic. It is especially good as the basis of a dip.

Crowdie   This very old recipe for a fresh cheese is still made by the crofters. It has been made in the Highlands and Islands since Viking and probably even Pictish times, and the name derives from the Gaelic *gruth*. It is unique in being the only semi-cooked cheese in the British Isles. The cheese makes a delicious salad and is very good served on oatcakes.

Now Let the Cheering Cup Be Poured

1880 regimental dinner of Lord Elcho and the London Scottish Volunteers

In Scotland as elsewhere festivals have evolved with the natural rhythms of life: from the farming year, the fluctuating fish stocks, the momentous events within the family such as births, christenings, weddings, burials. Many of the Feast Days have their origins in ancient Celtic rites and have been adapted over the centuries to man's changing beliefs and customs. The Festival of St Bride, for instance, on 1 February, derives from the worship of the pagan fire goddess Brid, and on St Bride's day the fishermen of Barra traditionally cast lots for their fishing grounds.

Countless superstitions have sprung up around these dates, the origins of many of which remain obscure. The Highlands and Western Islands in particular are rich in folklore, where even the days of the week were considered auspicious for certain daily practices and bad luck for others. I. F. Grant has collected some of these in his book *Highland Folk Ways*, and he discovered that Friday 'was not a good day to begin anything; it was unlucky to cut nails or hair, to kill a sheep or to begin to cut the hay, for buying anything or for being buried. It was, however, lucky for planting, sowing and for making bargains'.

Saints' days, too, kept their customs even after the Reformation. Special bannocks were baked on these days and the rich St Michael's Day bannock, which by tradition was made of the year's first grinding of grain, is still made on the islands of Barra and South Uist.

Perhaps the two most ancient festivals still known to us in some measure are Beltane and Samhain, the first days of May and November respectively, when the livestock were put out to pasture on the mountainside and returned to the farmstead for winter. Nowadays the

Two Tappit Hen measures, c. 1800

celebration of May Day has all but died out, although within living memory the special Beltane bannock was baked on this date. Pieces of this would be tossed over the herdsman's shoulder as an offering to the beasts and birds of prey which troubled their flocks, and whole bannocks were rolled down certain hillsides to foretell the future. Samhain, however, is still celebrated as Hallowe'en, and this day before All Saints' Day, which marks the onset of winter, is said to belong to the witches and is another example of a Christian festival amalgamating with an ancient heathen celebration.

Nowadays five festivals are primarily observed in the Scottish home: Christmas, Hogmanay or New Year, Burns' Night, St Andrew's Day and Hallowe'en. The Scots have ever been glad of the excuse for a feast, in contrast, perhaps, to the hardness and frugality of life in the past. It is indicative of the reverence in which these festivals were held that when in the sixteenth century a law was passed restricting extravagant eating because of food shortages, exemptions were granted for certain Feast Days and special celebrations.

The following menus are samples of the dishes served at each respective feast throughout the year.

You will find the recipes for some of the dishes in this chapter; the others can be located in other parts of the book.

Burns' Night

25 January
Cock-a-Leekie
Haggis with Tatties-an'-Neeps
Roastit Beef
Typsy Laird
Dunlop Cheese

Singing Auld Lang Syne *in a tavern: an early nineteenth century wood engraving*

Robbie Burns was Scotland's greatest poet, a poet of his people if ever there was one. He was born in Ayrshire on 25 January 1759, and each year his birth is celebrated with great pride and enthusiasm on this date. 'Burns' Nicht' is an informal, homely affair, and supper usually opens with the *Selkirk Grace*, which has been attributed to Burns:

> *Some hae meat, and canna eat,*
> *And some wad eat that want it,*
> *But we hae meat and we can eat,*
> *And sae the Lord be thankit.*

The haggis is always served accompanied by chappit tatties and bashed neeps, and it is traditionally washed down with neat whisky. This is only one of several courses, however, and after the soup or fish a member of the party is called upon ceremonially to address the haggis, in the form of verses from Burns' poem *Address to a Haggis*. The poet is then toasted with whisky, as is 'oor land', of which the Scot is so proud, and other songs and poems by Burns are recited.

Haggis

'Great Chieftain o' the puddin'-race!' was Burns' own description in his *Address to a Haggis*. The haggis is, in fact, nothing more than a rather unusual sausage, and the word probably derives from *hag*, meaning to chop or hack.

Nowadays I personally feel that the haggis you can buy is so good it is best not to make it yourself, and some of the ingredients are difficult to obtain unless you know a friendly butcher. However I thought you might like a recipe for haggis just in case you feel adventurous. I have adapted this particular recipe from one very kindly given to me by the Scotch Quality Beef and Lamb Association Limited.

the stomach bag and pluck (heart, liver and lights) of a sheep

2 onions, peeled

12 oz pinhead oatmeal (2 cups)

8 oz shredded suet (1⅔ cups)

salt and pepper

a trussing needle and fine string

Thoroughly wash the stomach bag in cold water. Turn it inside out and scald it, then scrape the surface with a knife. Soak it in cold salted water overnight. Next day remove the bag from the water and leave it on one side while preparing the filling.

Wash the pluck. Put it into a pan, with the windpipe hanging over the side into a bowl to let out any impurities. Cover the pluck with cold water, add 1 teaspoon of salt and bring the water to the boil. Skim the surface, then simmer for 1½–2 hours. Meanwhile parboil the onions, drain, reserving the liquid, and chop them roughly. Also toast the pinhead oatmeal until golden brown.

Drain the pluck when ready and cut away the windpipe and any excess gristle. Mince half the liver with all the heart and lights, then stir in the shredded suet, the toasted oatmeal and the onions. Season well with salt and pepper. Moisten with as much of the onion or pluck water as necessary to make the mixture soft.

With the rough surface of the bag outside fill it just over half full – the oatmeal will swell during cooking – and sew the ends together with the trussing needle and fine string. Prick the bag in places with the needle. Place the haggis on an enamel plate and put it into a pan of boiling water. Cover the pan and cook for about 3 hours, adding more boiling water when necessary to keep the haggis covered.

Serve with the traditional accompaniment of Tatties-an' Neeps – mashed potatoes and mashed turnips.

Hallowe'en

31 October
Chicken Pasties
Potted Beef Sandwiches
Hallowe'en Cake
Drambuie Cream
Crowdie Cheese and Apples

All Souls' Day, and the Gaelic festival of Samhain, marks the start of the dark, lean months of winter. Bonfires were lit to ward off evil spirits, and countless superstitions were attached to this particular date. A root of kail might be pulled and its size would indicate the stature of a future spouse; a girl might throw a rope over the kiln (for drying grain) and ask who caught it, and her future husband would answer; and the discovery of a coin in the traditional dish of cream and oatmeal foretold marriage for the finder. Nowadays Hallowe'en is an excuse for a party and a good opportunity for children to indulge in spooky fun. The centrepiece of the table is the Hallowe'en cake.

Potted Beef

6 oz cold cooked beef (1 cup)

4 oz cream cheese (½ cup)

1 level dessertspoon tomato purée (2 teaspoons)

1 level dessertspoon mayonnaise (2 teaspoons)

¼ level teaspoon French mustard

a good pinch of mace

1 oz melted butter (2 tablespoons)

This makes a very delicious sandwich filling. Depending on the thickness of filling you like it should be sufficient for about twelve rounds of bread. As butter is included in the recipe there is no need to butter the bread first.

Mince the beef and mix in the cream cheese. Stir in the tomato purée, mayonnaise, mustard and ground mace with salt if required. Pack the potted meat into a small dish. Cover the surface with a layer of melted butter if the filling is not to be used immediately. Keep in a cool place until required.

Facing page: Scottish Sparkle;
Manor Punch; Hilton Fling

Left: Atholl Brose Pudding

Chicken Pasties

Makes 9

1 14-oz packet frozen puff pastry (thawed)

a little beaten egg for glaze

For the filling

1 oz butter (2 tablespoons)

2 oz streaky bacon rashers

1 small onion, peeled and chopped

6 oz cooked chicken, chopped (1 cup)

1 oz plain flour ($\frac{1}{4}$ cup)

$\frac{1}{4}$ pint milk ($\frac{2}{3}$ cup)

Hallowe'en. The blindfolded person chooses one of three bowls: clean water indicates marriage to a young man or maid; dirty water marriage to a widow or widower; an empty bowl that they will die a batchelor or old maid

These pasties are just as good made with turkey, and this is also a useful recipe for Christmas leftovers.

Melt the butter in a pan. Remove the rind and any bones from the bacon and chop the rasher into small pieces. Add them to the pan with the onion and cook the ingredients together until soft but not coloured.

Remove the pan from the heat and stir in the flour, then gradually blend in the milk. Stirring all the time, bring the sauce to the boil and cook it for a minute to thicken. Stir in the chicken, then leave to cool.

Roll out the pastry thinly and cut out as many rounds as possible, using a $3\frac{1}{2}$-inch pastry cutter. Gather up the scraps, re-roll the dough and cut out more rounds to make 18 in all.

Divide the filling between 9 of them, moisten the edges of the remaining 9 and place them on top, sealing the edges well.

Put the pasties onto baking trays, brush with egg glaze and bake at Gas 7/425°F/220°C for 20–25 minutes or until well risen and golden brown.

Serve warm.

Hallowe'en Cake

The cake always takes pride of place on the buffet table at Hallowe'en. It is full of charms that tell fortunes especially those relating to marriage. A button is for single bliss, a ring for the first to marry, a wishbone for the heart's desire, and a horse-shoe for good luck.

At some parties the charms are embedded in a large bowl of steaming mashed potatoes, or at others, especially in the Highlands, the charms are hidden in furarag, a dish of oatmeal and buttermilk.

For the cake

8 oz butter (1 cup)

8 oz caster sugar (1 cup)

4 standard eggs (size 3)

12 oz self-raising flour (3 cups)

the grated rind of 1 orange

3 tablespoons milk

For the icing

¼ lb apricot jam (6 tablespoons)

1 lb sifted icing sugar (3¾ cups)

the juice of 1 orange

a little orange colouring

an 8-inch cake tin, greased and base lined

Beat the butter until soft, add the sugar and cream the two ingredients together to a soft and fluffy texture. Beat in the eggs one at a time, adding a little sifted flour if the mixture begins to curdle. Stir in the charms, wrapped in greaseproof paper, the orange rind with the milk and all the flour to make a soft dropping consistency. Turn the mixture into the tin and spread it to the sides, leaving the centre slightly hollow.

Bake the cake at Gas 4/350°F/180°C for 1–1¼ hours or until the cake is well risen, golden brown and slightly shrinking away from the sides of the tin. Leave the cake to cool.

To make the icing

Split the cake in half, spread it with the jam then sandwich the pieces back together and stand the cake on a wire tray.

Mix the orange juice with the icing sugar, adding warm water if necessary to make an icing that thickly coats the back of a spoon. Colour the icing orange then pour it over the cake, guiding it to the edges and letting it flow over the sides. Leave the cake to dry then decorate it with chocolate or black paper cut-outs of witches, cats, broomsticks etc.

St Andrew's Day

30 November
Bawd Bree
Haggis
Howtowdie with Chappit Tatties
Apple Frushie with Whippit Cream
Dunlop Cheese

The Patron Saint of Scotland is fêted on 30 November in true Scottish style. The most traditional of foods are served and patriotism runs high. The haggis may well be piped in with the bagpipes, and a lot of whisky is of course consumed. The entertainment is lively and Scottish reels are danced, and the party ends with the singing of *Auld Lang Syne*, another legacy from Robbie Burns. This is sung at the turn of the year in England, but in Scotland it concludes most festivities. The hands should be joined only at the start of the second verse.

The dining room at Hopetoun House, West Lothian

Bawd Bree

Serves 6

1 hare skinned and jointed – ask the butcher for the blood

1 teaspoon vinegar

1 oz lard (2 tablespoons)

1 tablespoon plain flour

8 oz shin of beef, chopped (1⅓ cups)

2 oz streaky bacon, chopped (⅓ cup)

2 medium onions, peeled and roughly chopped

1 turnip, peeled and roughly chopped

1 parsnip, peeled and roughly chopped

2 carrots, peeled and roughly chopped

4 pints water (10 cups)

6 peppercorns

4 cloves

1 bay leaf

1 tablespoon redcurrant jelly

a squeeze of lemon juice

2 tablespoons port

For the stuffing balls

the hare's liver

4 oz fresh breadcrumbs (¾ cup)

1 small onion, peeled and grated

1 oz butter (2 tablespoons)

a little milk

A superb soup for a festive occasion.

Mix the vinegar into the blood to prevent it clotting and leave on one side.

Melt the lard in a large pan, add the bacon and fry the pieces until they start to brown. Toss the hare joints in the flour seasoned with salt and pepper and brown them also in the fat. Transfer to a plate. Add all the vegetables and when they start to colour return the hare and bacon to the pan with the chopped beef. Pour in the water, add the peppercorns, cloves and bay leaf, then slowly bring the soup to the boil. Skim the surface, lower the heat and cook the soup covered for 2–3 hours or until the meat is tender.

Strain the soup and remove the hare joints. Take off all the meat and shred it finely. Rub the vegetables through a fine sieve back into the soup and stir through the hare meat. Bring the soup to the boil and add the redcurrant jelly and lemon juice. Strain the blood, pour a little of the hot soup into it, stirring all the time, then return it to the soup. Stir until just below boiling – if the soup boils it may curdle. Add the port and check for seasoning. Serve with the stuffing balls.

To make the stuffing balls

Melt the butter and fry the liver until cooked. Remove and chop finely. Stir the onion into the pan and when it starts to cook mix in the breadcrumbs, chopped liver, seasoning and enough stock to bind the mixture together. Divide it into small balls about the size of marbles, roll them in seasoned flour and fry till brown in a little extra butter.

Note: if you are unable to obtain a whole hare some shops sell hare joints – use 1 lb for the soup, then instead of the blood thicken the liquid with a buerre manié of 1 oz (2 tablespoons) butter to 2 tablespoons flour. Beat the ingredients together and stir them gradually into the soup so that they dissolve and thicken the liquid.

Christmas

25 December
Roastit Bubblyjock wi' Cheston Crappin
Plum Pudding
Mince Pies

Yuletide has never been celebrated in Scotland to the same extent as Hogmanay, and in some parts of the Highlands it used to be observed on what is known as Twelfth Night, 6 January, in accordance with the old calendar.

As might be expected there is a Yule bannock, which was divided into farls or quarters by the sign of the cross. The bannocks were apparently baked before dawn on the morning of Christmas day, and one given to each member of the family. If it could be kept intact until the evening meal this augured consistent good fortune for the coming year; if broken or nibbled, fortunes would break too. However, this round bannock, like so many others, has an earlier origin linked to Celtic sun worship.

Roastit Bubblyjock wi' Cheston Crappin

This marvellous title translated into English simply means Roast Turkey with Chestnut Stuffing. 'Bubblyjock' is probably imitative of the gobbling sound made by the turkey.

Prepare the turkey on Christmas Eve by first removing the giblets, which can then be made into stock or Giblet Pie (see page 67). Weigh the bird and calculate the cooking time at 20 minutes to the pound plus 20 minutes.

Mix the chestnut purée with the breadcrumbs. Stir in the suet and add the onion, parsley and lemon rind and plenty of seasoning. Bind the ingredients together with the egg

Serves 10
a 10-lb turkey
2 oz butter (¼ cup)

For the stuffing
1 lb chestnuts, cooked, peeled and puréed *or* 1 15-oz can unsweetened chestnut purée
4 oz fresh brown breadcrumbs (¾ cup)
2 oz prepared shredded suet (6 tablespoons)
1 medium onion, peeled and grated
1 level tablespoon chopped parsley
the grated rind of 1 lemon
1 standard egg (size 3), beaten

then, starting at the neck end of the bird, work your hand under the skin until half way along the breast. Insert the stuffing under the breast skin pressing it well into the shape of the bird. Retruss the turkey and keep it cool until ready to cook.

Melt the butter in a roasting tin, add the turkey and baste. Loosely cover the tin with foil and roast the bird at Gas 4/350°F/180°C for the calculated cooking time. Remove the foil for the last $\frac{3}{4}$ hour so as to brown the bird.

Serve the turkey with chipolata sausages, bacon rolls, bread sauce, roast potatoes and brussels sprouts.

Plum Pudding

8 oz cleaned currents ($1\frac{1}{4}$ cups)

8 oz cleaned sultanas ($1\frac{1}{4}$ cups)

8 oz stoned and chopped raisins ($1\frac{1}{4}$ cups)

4 oz mixed peel, chopped ($\frac{3}{4}$ cup)

4 oz blanched, browned and chopped almonds ($\frac{2}{3}$ cup)

8 oz fresh white breadcrumbs ($1\frac{1}{2}$ cups)

8 oz soft brown sugar (1 cup, firmly packed)

8 oz prepared shredded suet ($1\frac{2}{3}$ cups)

the finely grated rind and juice of 1 lemon

8 oz plain flour (2 cups)

a pinch of salt

1 level teaspoon ground nutmeg

1 level teaspoon ground cinnamon

1 level teaspoon mixed spice

3 large eggs (size 2), beaten

$\frac{1}{2}$ pint brown ale or stout ($1\frac{1}{4}$ cups)

Plum (Christmas) Puddings take two days to make. On the first day mix all the dry ingredients and bind them together to make the pudding. On the second day turn the mixture into the basin and steam it. This recipe makes one large pudding cooked in a 3-pint pudding basin or two smaller puddings.

Mix the dried fruit together with the peel and almonds. Stir in the sugar, breadcrumbs, suet and lemon rind.

Sift together the flour and spices then mix them into the other ingredients with the eggs, lemon juice and stout to make a fairly soft consistency. Leave overnight.

Next day turn the pudding mixture into one greased 3-pint basin or two smaller ones and spread it level. Cover with a doubled sheet of greased greaseproof paper and make a pleat across the top to allow the pudding to rise. Fasten the cover with string then steam the pudding, about 8 hours for the large one, 6 hours for the smaller ones. Do not forget to replenish the pan with more boiling water when necessary. Leave the pudding to cool.

Re-cover each pudding with fresh greaseproof paper and store in a cool dry place until required. It will keep for up to a year.

Plum pudding is reheated by steaming it for at least 2 hours or until heated through.

A Choice of Mince Pies

The first recipe makes short and crumbly pies, while the second gives a flaky texture.

Crumbly Mince Pies

Makes 12

10 oz plain flour (2½ cups)

a good pinch of salt

3 oz margarine (6 tablespoons)

2 oz lard (¼ cup)

¾ lb mincemeat (1½ cups, firmly packed)

Sift the flour and salt into a bowl. Add the fats cut into small pieces and rub them in until evenly distributed. Stir in sufficient cold water to make a fairly stiff dough, then knead it lightly on a floured surface. Roll the dough out to a thickness of about one-eighth of an inch and cut out an even quantity of 3-inch and 2-inch rounds. Line tartlet tins with the larger rounds, fill with mincemeat and cover with the smaller rounds, sticking the lids securely in place with water. Re-roll any pastry trimmings to make more mince pies. Make a hole in the centre of each with a skewer and bake the pies at Gas 6/400°F/200°C for about 20 minutes.

Cool, then dust with icing sugar before serving.

Flaky Mince Pies

Makes 12

8 oz plain flour (2 cups)

a pinch of salt

6 oz hard margarine (¾ cup)

1 teaspoon lemon juice

¾ lb mincemeat (1½ cups, firmly packed)

a little caster sugar

Sift the flour and salt into a bowl. Coarsely grate in the margarine, mix it through the flour and bind the ingredients together with the lemon juice and sufficient cold water to make a fairly stiff dough. Roll it out on a floured surface to an oblong then fold it into three, i.e. the top third over the middle third and the bottom third up over the other two thirds. Seal the edges, then leave the dough to rest for 15 minutes.

Roll it out to a thickness of one-eighth of an inch and continue as for Crumbly Mince Pies.

Before baking, brush the surface of each with water and dust with caster sugar. Bake the pies at Gas 6/400°F/200°C for 20–30 minutes or until golden brown.

Serve warm.

Hogmanay

31 December
Kipper Cream
Ayrshire Bacon
Salads
Black Bun
Shortbread

The celebration of the New Year belongs most truly to the Scot. The origin of the word Hogmanay is lost, though it may come from the old French *aguil' anneuf*, meaning 'to the New Year'. The custom of first footing derives from the good fairy of Norse folklore. At midnight the men folk set off to first foot their neighbours, and the first man to cross the threshold of a home in the New Year is the first foot. Each one carries a bottle of whisky and some thin oatcakes and the householder is offered a dram for good luck. Refreshment of more whisky or Atholl Brose, shortbread or Scotch Bun are offered in return. If a dark haired man is the first foot this augurs well for the year; a red-head is unlucky, as is a woman.

Kipper Cream

Serves 8

1 lb kipper fillets, cooked

½ pint milk (1¼ cups)

1 oz butter (2 tablespoons)

1 oz plain flour (¼ cup)

¼ pint mayonnaise (⅔ cup)

2 large eggs (size 2) separated

1 dessertspoon lemon juice

a pinch of nutmeg

½ oz powdered gelatine
(2 US envelopes)

3 tablespoons water

Remove the skins from the kippers and flake the fish.

Melt the butter, stir in the flour, remove from the heat and blend in the milk. Bring to the boil, stirring constantly, then stir in the egg yolks, nutmeg and lemon juice.

Dissolve the gelatine in the water, stir it into the sauce with the kippers and leave on one side until starting to set.

Quickly whisk the egg whites, then fold them into the sauce with the mayonnaise. Turn the mixture into a shallow 2-pint dish, lightly oiled. Smooth over the surface and leave overnight to set.

Next day turn onto a serving plate and garnish with cucumber slices and green stuffed olives.

Black Bun

For the pastry

12 oz plain flour (3 cups)

a pinch of salt

3 oz lard (6 tablespoons)

3 oz margarine (6 tablespoons)

For the filling

1 lb seedless raisins (2¾ cups)

1 lb cleaned currants (2¾ cups)

2 oz blanched chopped almonds (⅓ cup)

2 oz mixed peel, chopped (¼ cup)

6 oz plain flour (1½ cups)

3 oz soft brown sugar (⅓ cup)

1 level teaspoon ground allspice

½ level teaspoon ground ginger

½ level teaspoon ground cinnamon

a pinch of black pepper

½ level teaspoon baking powder

1 tablespoon brandy

1 large egg (size 2), beaten

milk to moisten

an 8-inch loaf tin, greased

This festive Hogmanay cake is also known as Scotch Bun, and was originally eaten on Twelfth Night. Make the bun at least two weeks before it is required, and sooner still if possible. In fact it will remain fresh for up to six months if stored in an airtight tin.

Sift the flour and salt into a bowl, rub in the fats, then mix in enough cold water to make a fairly stiff dough. Roll out three quarters of it and line the sides and base of the tin.

Mix the raisins, currants, almonds, chopped peel and sugar together. Sift in the flour, ground allspice, ginger, cinnamon, pepper and baking powder. Then bind the ingredients together using the brandy, almost all the beaten egg (leaving a little for the glaze) and enough milk just to moisten.

Pack the filling into the lined tin, then roll out the remaining piece of dough and use it for the lid. Seal the edges really well together, lightly prick the surface with a fork and make four holes right through to the bottom using a skewer.

Brush the surface with egg glaze then bake the bun at Gas 3/325°F/160°C for 3 hours. Cool in the tin then store until Hogmanay.

The Toast of Scotland

To complement its meat, game, fruit and fish, Scotland has a wealth of appetizing drinks. The two best known are of course whisky and the famous Drambuie liqueur, and a little about the origin of these will be found in the Introduction to this book. They are delicious on their own and also make excellent bases for cocktails and punches. Each has a characteristic Scottish flavour. Here are a few recipes, some bound up in the traditions and history of the country, others that I think are just good to drink. I hope you agree.

Atholl Brose

This old Scottish beverage is a favourite drink to offer first footers. It is thought to have originated in 1475 when the Earl of Atholl captured the Earl of Ross by filling the well at which he was wont to drink with this potent concoction.

Atholl Brose has with time developed many versions. Here is one that I hope is as near to the original as possible. Do try the luscious dessert version on page 144.

3 rounded tablespoons medium oatmeal

2 tablespoons heather honey

whisky

Mix the oatmeal with enough cold water to make a thin paste. Leave the mixture to stand for half an hour, then strain it through a sieve, pressing it well down so the meal becomes quite dry again. Discard the meal.   Mix the liquid with the honey and stir with a silver spoon until well mixed.

Pour the liquid into a quart bottle and fill up with whisky. Cork and shake well before serving.

Het Pint

This drink is associated with Hogmanay as it was always served on New Year's morning. It was also drunk on the night before a wedding or a lying-in.

Serves 6–8

4 pints pale ale (10 cups)

1 level teaspoon freshly grated nutmeg

sugar to taste

3 standard eggs (size 3)

$\frac{1}{2}$ pint whisky ($1\frac{1}{4}$ cups)

Pour the ale into a large pan, add the nutmeg and bring the liquid to just below boiling. Stir in enough sugar to taste. In a large bowl beat the eggs then very gradually stir in the hot ale. If the liquid is added too quickly the eggs will curdle. Stir in the whisky, then pour the liquid back into the pan. Stirring constantly, bring the drink back to just below boiling point, then pour back and forth from a height in warmed tankards until the drink froths and becomes clear and sparkling.

Facing page: This is one of the most important glass goblets made to commemorate the Jacobite rebellion of 1745. The rosebuds represent the Pretenders, and the mottoes are significant: Turno Tempus Erit, *'events will be changed', and* Redeat, *'may he return'*

Hot Toddy

This warming drink is a good cure for a cold. If it is served for this purpose a tablespoon of lemon juice is often added.

1 measure of whisky
1 scant teaspoon sugar

Pour the whisky into a warmed glass, add the sugar and, using a silver spoon, stir in boiling water as required. Drink at once.

Mulled Wine

Sufficient for 20 glasses
1 pint water (2½ cups)
a 3-inch piece of cinnamon stick
1 level teaspoon ground nutmeg
3 oz soft brown sugar (⅓ cup)
2 oranges
3 bottles red wine
¼ pint Drambuie (⅔ cup)

Put the water, cinnamon stick, nutmeg and sugar into a pan. Thinly peel the rind from the oranges with a potato peeler and add it to the pan with the orange juice. Dissolve the sugar over a low heat, bring the liquid to the boil and then remove the pan from the heat. Leave it on one side for the flavours to infuse, for at least 15 minutes.
    Add the wine and Drambuie, then very slowly heat the liquid again: do not allow it to boil.
    Keep the mulled wine on a low heat and serve in warmed glasses.

Hilton Fling

1 measure Dubonnet
½ measure Drambuie
dash of orange bitters

Mix the Dubonnet and Drambuie together. Add a dash of orange bitters and a twist of orange.

Manor Punch

1 measure malt whisky
1 measure Martini Bianco
a dash of Drambuie

Stir the whisky, Martini and Drambuie together, strain into a glass and serve with a cherry.

Rusty Nails

1 measure Drambuie
1 measure whisky

Stir together and serve in a liqueur glass. This is an excellent after-dinner drink.

Scottish Sparkle

Serves 12
1 bottle dry white wine
1 bottle sparkling white wine
the juice of 1 lemon
¼ pint Drambuie (⅔ cup)
¾ pint lemonade (2 cups)

This drink is especially good on a warm summer's evening.

Mix the dry white wine, lemon juice and Drambuie together in a jug and chill, then at the last minute add the sparkling wine and lemonade.

Float pink and white rose petals on the surface and add plenty of ice to the punch before serving.

Café au Drambuie

Serves 1
3 dessertspoons Drambuie
(7 teaspoons)
1 level dessertspoon brown sugar
(2 teaspoons)
freshly made strong coffee
double cream

A perfect way to round off a meal.

Heat a stemmed glass in hot water and dry quickly. Add the Drambuie, stir in the sugar and pour in enough coffee to come within 1 inch of the rim. Stir the liquid until the sugar dissolves, then with the tip of a teaspoon just on the surface of the coffee pour the cream over the back of it so that the cream floats on the surface to a depth of half an inch. Serve at once.

Picture acknowledgements

Black-and-white photographs
K. M. Andrew: 80, 131. The British Tourist Authority: 96. Cecil Davis Ltd: 171.
The Mansell Collection: 108, 111, 133. Mary Evans Picture Library: endpapers, 15, 22,
47, 109, 156, 161. Oscar Marzaroli: 29, 110. The National Trust for Scotland: 27, 56,
89, 103, 114, 115. Radio Times Hulton Picture Library: 154. Scottish Field:
28, 48, 49, 127. Scottish Tourist Board: 24, 31, 85, 100, 121, 163. Sotheby Parke Bernet
& Co., London: 20, 21, 83 (above), 155.

Colour photographs
Courtesy of The Drambuie Liqueur Company Limited (photographs supplied by ADS
Marketing and Design Consultants Ltd): 17, 35, 72, 141. Courtesy of the Scottish
Quality Beef and Lamb Association: 54. Scottish Tourist Board: 18.

The remaining colour photographs were specially taken for the book by Jon Harris of
Guyatt/Jenkins.

The publishers wish to thank the following for their assistance: The Conran Shop,
London; Craftsmen and Potters Association of Great Britain; Garrard, the Crown
Jewellers; The Merchant Chandler Ltd, London; Searcy's; Josiah Wedgwood & Sons
Ltd.

Index